The Metaphysics of Ping-Pong

The Metaphysics of Ping-Pong

Table Tennis as a Journey of
Self-Discovery and the Spinning Ball
as our Planet Earth

Guido Mina di Sospiro

YELLOW JERSEY PRESS
LONDON

Published by Yellow Jersey Press 2013

2 4 6 8 10 9 7 5 3 1

Copyright © Guido Mina di Sospiro 2013

Guido Mina di Sospiro has asserted his right under the Copyright, Designs
and Patents Act 1988 to be identified as the author of this work

First published in Great Britain in 2013 by
Yellow Jersey Press
Random House, 20 Vauxhall Bridge Road,
London SW1V 2SA

www.vintage-books.co.uk

Addresses for companies within The Random House Group Limited can be
found at: www.randomhouse.co.uk/offices.htm

The Random House Group Limited Reg. No. 954009

A CIP catalogue record for this book
is available from the British Library

ISBN 9780224092166

The Random House Group Limited supports the Forest Stewardship Council®
(FSC®), the leading international forest-certification organisation. Our books
carrying the FSC label are printed on FSC®-certified paper. FSC is the only
forest-certification scheme supported by the leading environmental organisations,
including Greenpeace. Our paper procurement policy can be found at
www.randomhouse.co.uk/environment

Typeset in Bembo by Palimpsest Book Production Limited,
Falkirk, Stirlingshire
Printed and bound in Great Britain by
Clays Ltd, St Ives plc

To my wife Stenie,

with reverent gratitude for allowing me to live
with her on Mount Parnassus.

Contents

Prelude

When I was a child I used to go to a summer camp in the Dolomites, a mountain range in the Alps in north-eastern Italy. We boys and girls played, hiked, picnicked, flirted and enjoyed the great outdoors and the invigorating mountain air, which gave us voracious appetites. When it rained, we were corralled into a huge recreation room on the first floor of the building, with large windows looking out towards the mountains. In it there was a single ping-pong table, access to which was determined by the Draconian rule of 'winner stays.'

One boy, a little older than most of us – fourteen or fifteen – was clearly the best player. No matter how much we tried, he would spend every rainy day at the table, undefeated. He wielded a Butterfly – a high-quality Japanese racket – with the 'mythical' Sriver inverted rubbers. Unlike most other rackets in that recreation room, the rubber on the Sriver had the characteristic pimples *in*, leaving the smooth side of the topsheet to strike the ball. We, on the other hand, played with whatever was available. It was the 1970s, 'Made in Japan' was invading the world and certainly occupying almost militarily that ping-pong table high up in the Dolomites in the hand of that skilful player. It's curious how I don't remember his name but do remember his equipment so clearly. Indeed the Butterfly Sriver *is* a mythical rubber. Thanks to many updates and new incarnations, it is still used at the highest levels. Introduced in 1967, this rubber was off to a very good start, having quickly become the weapon of choice for advanced players. Today, more than twenty World and seventy European Champions have won their titles with Sriver.

I asked the player wielding the Japanese racket where he had bought it and, I recall vividly, he said that he had bought the 'blade' (which back then sounded menacing, but it's only the portion of the racket to which the rubbers are attached) in one place, the rubbers in another, and then had glued them onto the blade and cut the rubbers precisely to size. This sounded fantastical to me. 'You've done all that? Really?' I said, in disbelief.

He looked at me superciliously.

I pressed on: 'What for? Why make one step into two? Why didn't you buy it ready-made?'

'You mean, *preassembled*?' yet more superciliously.

Is that what it's called? I wondered in my mind and said: 'Yes, of course, pre-as-sem-bled.'

He frowned as he replied, '*We* don't bother with those . . .' and moved away, visibly annoyed by both my impertinence and my ignorance.

The Butterfly Sriver would not by itself improve my game, but it *was* a marvel. Not that I ever got one, but another, lesser Butterfly I did manage to buy. And with it I began to experiment.

Once into my teens, I no longer went to the summer camp in the mountains, but to the sea instead. I remember a ping-pong table there, in the shade of a large magnolia tree. My hand, aided by my new racket, began to learn not only to push the ball across the net, but how to make it travel across the air while rotating. The effect as it touched the table was, I thought, amazing. I was learning some basic spins, which I'd test on a more or less willing guinea pig, my sister. She would expect the ball to bounce normally on her side of the table and instead it would bounce *sideways*, to the left or to the right, and she would miss it. Later, I learned to make the ball bounce *up* more than expected, or to backspin it so that my sister would return it invariably into the net, much to her frustration. She and other beginners thought that it was magic, while I enjoyed passing for a magician.

So my earliest approach to ping-pong was *not* inspired by speed. Not that speed doesn't have its role in ping-pong – and how! – but back then it seemed to me that there was tennis for that, with brawny people running around a big court grunting in the sun. No, what caught my imagination, and still does, was spin. Without knowing it, I was on the right track, as the consensus nowadays is that ping-pong is first and foremost a game of spin.

My friends never seemed to take ping-pong seriously. Chasing girls, a spin on a motorcycle, going to the beach – all other activities seemed preferable to them. I would have liked to play more and improve, but committed players were hard to come by. Ping-pong was a summer pastime, to be played outdoors. For the rest of the year, we didn't see a racket.

Ping-pong lay dormant inside me. From time to time I would revive it. At eighteen I spent a month in the summer in a Swiss *collège* high up in the Bernese Alps. Among the kids there were a few enthusiastic ping-pongers. We found an open-air, all-weather table made of concrete. Between the very hard surface, the thin air and the slightly smaller ball that was used then, our rallies were ridiculously fast. Add occasional wind gusts that made the ball swerve unpredictably, and the effect was exhilarating, and surreal, too. Picture the setting: a table surrounded by glistening snow-capped peaks under the strongest sun with Holstein cows mooing and grazing nearby on the steepest slopes. We used to play all day and drink, in the pre-Gatorade days, Coca-Cola mixed with ice-cold water that came straight from the glaciers. Then, a life-changing move: from Milan to Los Angeles, to attend the University of Southern California.

For years I didn't even come close to a racket, not by choice, but because my time was taken up by so many other things, and I had met, and later married, the love of my life, a girl from rival UCLA.

A few years later we became parents and moved to Miami. Eventually I bought a ping-pong table, which I placed *not* in the basement – there are no basements in South Florida – but under the carport. I immediately set about teaching the game to our three boys. They learned quickly and were soon playing well enough, but after some months their interest waned. Forcing them to play was just wrong, and I couldn't find challenging opponents. So, since I hated seeing the table unutilised, I reluctantly gave it away.

But we did have one in our house in Italy, as is typical outdoors. During a summer some years ago our friend Rupert Sheldrake – the controversial philosopher of science – his wife Jill and their two boys, Merlin and Cosmos, paid us a visit. I gave the boys rackets and showed them a few strokes. It was instant karma: they were hooked. Back in London, they persuaded their father to buy them a table and he himself has become a player. Every time I went to visit them there were the inevitable ping-pong matches. I'd play for hours with both sons and with Rupert, too. It was fun and, surprisingly, also intellectually stimulating. There was something unusual about the essence of the game that escaped us. Eventually, after some speculative discussions about it, we realised what was intriguing us: the fact that ping-pong is strikingly non-Euclidean. I have kept a note that he sent me about it: 'Euclidean geometry is the geometry of plain surfaces and three-dimensional space, but non-Euclidean geometry is the geometry of curved surfaces, hence it is indeed an appropriate term for this kind of ping-pong.'

What I took as an official confirmation of my ability as a player came six years ago, on a cruise ship. A ping-pong tournament had been organised. Half-hoping that this would happen, I had brought along my (still preassembled and seldom used) racket. I had just discovered that on a cruise three new factors further complicate the game: the rocking of the ship, the wind on deck and the . . . *margaritas*. But the tournament was held while the ship was still docked; in a sheltered spot undisturbed by wind; and no alcohol was served on board while in port. The tournament turned out to be uneventful: no opponent gave me a hard time and I won.

So, even if I no longer owned a table and played rarely, ping-pong seemed to catch up with me constantly. By the time it did for good, it suited me all the more because meanwhile I had been cultivating the art of thinking unconventionally. During my university years, first in Pavia then in LA at USC, between classes I'd go to one of the libraries on campus and read – avidly – the *Encyclopædia Britannica* at random. Everything interested me, but ultimately nothing satisfied me. Disappointed by the canon taught at school and broadcast by the media and the establishment, by the time I graduated I was already delving well beyond it. For years I've been exploring a different kind of knowledge. Sufism, for example, shows one how to escape from the 'prisons of linear thinking.' And so, in different ways, do Taoism and Zen.

To illustrate an instance of escape from the 'prisons of linear thinking,' I won't use a passage from some ancient esoteric text, but a TV commercial for 'Instant Kiwi,' a lottery scratch card from New Zealand – sometimes this kind of thinking hides itself in the most unsuspected places.

Students are taking an exam. A rather pompous professor is watching them while the clock is ticking. 'Time, thank you,' he eventually says. 'Put down your pens and bring your papers to the front of the room.' All students do so but one; he's wasting time scratching an instant lottery ticket, but he could be finishing the exam. This one student reaches the desk to turn in the exam past the allotted time. The professor says: 'I'm sorry, too late.'

The student is dumbfounded.

'I gave you plenty of warnings about time,' resumes the professor. 'You failed. Sorry.'

'Excuse me,' says the student in a matter-of-fact tone, 'do you know who I am?'

The professor, contemptuously: 'I have absolutely no idea.'

'Good,' says the student, and places his paper in the middle of the stack.

This catches us by surprise. But it's more than surprising; it's mind-bending. One feels that logic is being violated, and with it the laws of linear thinking. To be totally unknown is very desirable. In fact, thanks to his anonymity, the student still manages to hand in his exam. Furthermore, the professor is making the wrong assumption as he replies to the student. In fact, *he*, the professor, is being tested, and *he* is the one who fails.

Down the centuries Taoism, Zen and Sufism have created a large repertoire of short and seemingly mundane stories whose goal is that of violating logics and challenging our assumptions. Twentieth-century traditionalists have done much of the same, by turning received notions upside down. Ping-pong, as I will show, has so many baffling and refreshingly illogical qualities about it that, whenever I happened to play an occasional game, somehow it echoed inside me in a new and increasingly resonant way. And as a result of that I marvelled all the more at how magical it was to spin that little ball and make it fly, bounce on the table *and* off the opponent's racket in mysterious ways.

1

True Beginnings, and Shock and Awe

My full-blown obsession with ping-pong began four years ago with the semi-epic road trip. 'Semi' because my original idea was to drive during the summer from Washington, DC, to where we had moved, all the way to California and back – with two teenage sons in tow. But then my wife decided that we'd fly to Albuquerque, New Mexico, rent a car there, and drive all over the south-west, eventually into Southern California, and then north to San Francisco, where we'd drop off the car and fly back.

The boys, glued to their smartphones, texted away with abandon, or dozed through most of the natural wonders, only to wake up in Las Vegas, and keep wide-awake in LA, Santa Barbara and all the way north along the precipitous Pacific Coast Highway in anticipation of San Francisco.

In Big Sur we chanced upon the Henry Miller Memorial Library, which instantly rang a bell. I hadn't forgotten how much the writer had amused me with his 'forbidden book' *Tropic of Cancer*, engaged me with *The Colossus of Maroussi* and surprised me, later on, with certain passages in *Big Sur and the Oranges of Hieronymus Bosch*. And here we were, in Big Sur.

I should have been content with the awe-inspiring redwoods, the writer's memorabilia, and the welcoming and quirky people at the library. My wife was. But in the shade of the towering trees I could not miss a ping-pong table. 'Yes,' a young librarian told me when I asked her about it, 'Henry Miller was a good player. Back in nineteen sixty-three, for example, when he met with Bob Dylan, well . . . they didn't really hit it off.'

'No?'

'No, Henry found Dylan arrogant, and Dylan found Henry patronising. But guess what? They did play ping-pong. Ping-pong has always attracted clever people, you know?'

I didn't, but it was flattering to the sport and nice to hear.

'For example,' she continued, 'when the composer Arnold Schoenberg moved from Austria to Hollywood to escape from the Nazis, he used to play ping-pong with his neighbour, George Gershwin. In fact, Schoenberg used to go around with a violin case, only there was no violin in it, but a ping-pong bat.'

How about that, I thought. All this talk about ping-pong had definitively whetted my appetite. 'Would it be possible to play a little?' I asked her, pointing at the table in the distance.

'Sure. Here, take these bats, and here's the ball.'

'Thank you,' I said, looking at a more than ordinarily beaten-up ball and two vintage hardbats with their rubbers half peeled-off.

'Excuse me,' I said, 'but these wouldn't by chance be the bats Henry Miller himself played with?'

'Oh no, they couldn't be *that* old.'

They certainly looked it, but never mind. It seemed only natural that I should challenge Pietro, our then-eighteen-year-old son. He accepted the challenge with a smirk on his face. We'll see about that in a minute, I thought.

As we reached the table, I took a better look at the hardbats. A hardbat is a racket that uses short outward pimples ('pips') with no sponge between the rubber and the wood of the blade. As it belongs to a much earlier era in the history of the sport, I had never played with it. Didn't somebody say, 'Never play unless you have your own racket?' Maybe, but why so much caution? I would beat Pietro easily, and teach him a lesson, too.

The match began, and quickly went downhill for me. I was trying my spinny serves, but to no avail. My back-spinned chops, too, but they seemed to have no effect on his returns. My topspins had nothing on them. He, on the other hand, didn't bother with any fancy movement, but simply hammered the poor ball whenever he could. He easily won the first game.

As for the second game, he was leading by a wide margin despite all my efforts, when with one of his smashes he cracked the ball. I took the hint, and didn't ask the librarian for another one, but just returned the bats. 'Why didn't you ask her for another ball? I'd play on,' Pietro said.

'Nah, that's enough.'

'Fine by me, but this means that you withdrew from the match, so I've won.'

'Yes, yes, you've won.'

Indeed, he and the redwoods had had the last laugh: *he* had beaten me, and taught *me* a lesson. With his no-nonsense, flat ping-pong he had easily done away with all my attempts at spin. The orange ball had kept dodging me, as if Henry Miller himself had been throwing the oranges of Hieronymus Bosch – the visionary and wild Early Netherlandish painter – at me, but only rarely close enough for my decrepit bat to make contact. But Pietro's bat was just as decrepit; there was no excuse.

Shamed in defeat, I didn't contemplate hara-kiri, but did wonder, how on Earth could I have lost? It seemed inconceivable given my experience, but he'd beaten me soundly. Whatever . . . It was time to drive on, and I left it at that, or so I thought.

A month later I had a routine check-up at the doctor's and the diagnosis was high blood pressure. Not uncommon in men of my age, but still something that needed my attention. Physical exercise was prescribed.

Physical exercise? I'd never liked it in the least, but I did like walking. 'Walking is fine,' said the doctor; 'make it a couple of miles a day if you can, and walk briskly.'

Walking on a treadmill was the most efficient and precise way to follow up on the doctor's recommendation but, as it turned out, it was also dehumanising: the more miles I walked without arriving anywhere, the more I felt like a mule pulling a grindstone around endlessly. Still, I needed to exercise. What to do?

Apart from skiing, the only sport I'd enjoyed in my youth was ping-pong. They are at the opposite ends of the scale: the former one of the most expensive sports, the latter one of the cheapest. Skiing is seasonal and can hardly be practised every day even when in season. Ping-pong is much more manageable, can be played all year round, and I still hadn't really metabolised the beating my son had given me in California. But I'd learned that buying a table and setting it up at home wouldn't work. No, I needed a place in which people were eager to play. My son Nico suggested I consult the popular oracle – Google – for the nearest ping-pong place. I did, and was given the address of a community centre nearby. I asked Nico to accompany me. There we went – and stepped into a circus.

The characters clustered around three tables: half a dozen Chinese men in their late twenties, thirties and forties, all with a very strong accent. A taciturn – or mute? – Iranian in his sixties, thickset and perfectly bald, with a racket that harked back to the 1940s, much like the ones at Henry Miller's place (one side of it, as I eventually discovered; the other side was something entirely different, but at the time I couldn't know that). A Russian jock dressed in vest and shorts like a teenager but with a thick crown of grey hair. A few Americans, with two college students among them, one beset by physical tics. And to top it all, a Cuban in his late seventies, thin as a rake, who played as if glued to the table to obtain maximum results from minimum effort. Later I was to learn that he is a man of letters, the Treasurer of the North American Academy of the Spanish Language, a Corresponding Member of the Royal Spanish Academy, a Member of the Academy of the History of Cuba, and a grandson of the poetess Emilia Bernal Agüero, the grande dame of Cuban literature. Back then, bony, angular and sinister-looking, he reminded me of a character I had met in my childhood in the Italian comic book *Zagor*: Hellingen, the quintessence of all mad scientists, with the same domed bald head, shock of white hair and fierce gaze.

One of the Chinese players, a pudgy little man who couldn't stop talking as we waited for the room to clear from a yoga class, played with the typical Chinese penhold (with the racket held as a pen), and used only one face of his racket. When the Chinese played among themselves, they spoke in Mandarin, shouted and jumped around like uproarious crickets – on speed. While the thought of a cricket on speed is disconcerting enough in itself, the things they did with the ball belonged, in my view, more to the realm of magic. When I played them, I couldn't 'read' their strokes because I'd never played with penholders. I could more or less read the strokes of a shakehand grip opponent, which means that I (hope to) know in advance what kind of spin he gives to the ball, so as to know how to counter it. But the thing about these Chinese players is that they were no jocks at all: they reminded me more of comic acrobats. They laughed, shouted, leaped about, and played some mean ping-pong.

And what about the mute Iranian? He chiefly played defensively. A designated victim of the hyperactive Chinese funambulists? On the contrary: for reasons that I didn't understand then, he held his own and they could not beat him.

When it came to playing with the Cuban – Emilio – he made writhing faces of excruciating pain as if every time he served he were unleashing the wrath of God. The facial expressions alone were enough to make me wonder if I shouldn't run for my life. But then he forced me to scamper from one side of the table to the other like car wipers in a rainstorm and I inevitably lost the point. There I stood, beaten by a man pushing eighty . . .

Moreover, I'd gone there wearing a pair of slacks and a shirt, thinking that at most I'd roll up my sleeves, but doubting that I'd need to. I did have my seldom-used racket with me, and with it my spins would be deadly; so no need to run around, I'd presumed. In fact, I was soon bathed in sweat, slipping in moccasins, and cursing my hubris.

Never had I imagined that ping-pong could be whatever it was that was being practised in that room. I was both shocked and awed by what I experienced.

'What do we have here?' I asked the equally nonplussed Nico when the allotted two hours were over. 'A physics-defying discipline that requires feline reflexes played divinely by Chinese jesters with a hold so unnatural, their arm and wrist ache with their every shot!' My loss to Pietro paled in comparison to the beatings I'd taken. And to think that I'd gone there assuming that I wouldn't sweat a drop and would beat anybody easily – poor deluded fool. They hadn't just beaten me, they'd trampled all over me, as if I weren't on the other side of the table at all.

Above all, the amount of spin these players placed on the ball was shocking. Never had I experienced anything like it. When I played with them, the ball bounced off the table and off my racket, *if* I managed to reach it, in the most incredible ways. I spent more time collecting balls off the floor than playing. Extreme spin didn't only alter the trajectory and the bounce, but also increased the speed. And the speed they produced was another shock.

This was not the ping-pong I knew. Better yet: I obviously did *not* know the game. For years I'd only skimmed the surface, while these punishment inflictors had taken the plunge. The question arose of its own accord: what is 'table tennis,' as it's officially called? What is the true nature and essence of the game?

2
The Sandwich Revolution

A fter that demolition party, research was in order and, burning with curiosity, I delved straight in.

Table tennis began as a diversion for the upper class in Victorian England to mimic lawn tennis. Some say that, at first, players used books as rackets, others cigar-box lids with balls made of cork or solid rubber. Later, the rackets became drum battledores. Due to the lack of control, table tennis – or whiff-whaff, Gossima, ping-pong – at this stage was hardly a sport. 1900, however, was a seminal year, as the hollow celluloid ball was introduced. Hardbats became the typical racket – the same bats used by Miller, Schoenberg and Gershwin, among millions of others – and the game remained virtually unaltered for over half a century, dominated by European and American players. Then, at the 1952 World Championships in Bombay, Asia entered the scene. After training behind closed doors, Japan's least talented player on the team, bespectacled and unassuming Hiroji Satoh, unveiled his secret weapon: the sponge racket – a wooden blade covered on both sides in thick foam. It was formidable.

First of all, it made no sound when it hit the ball, which in itself was very disorienting. There was 'ping' on one side of the table, but no 'pong' on the other. But most of all, it produced unprecedented amounts of spin and speed: the ball would sink into the foam and be catapulted back. No conventional hardbat player could cope with this, and Hiroji Satoh won the World Championship.

What radically changed the sport for good, ushering in a long period of dominance by Asian players, occurred in 1954, in London, with Ichiro Ogimura's triumph as he won both the men's singles and team titles at the World Championship. It was the first of five straight championships he won in the men's team competition. During his career, Ogimura captured twelve world titles in singles, mixed doubles and team competitions. All Japanese team members by then were playing with foam-covered rackets, the same sponge racket that had been pioneered by Satoh. Until the early 1950s, the game had consisted of low parables with the ball just clearing the net and landing on the deep end of the table. Speed and placement were of the essence. The topspin movement was already utilised, but mainly to make the stroke more precise and consistent. The new racket revolutionised all this. Topspin would no longer be a stroke stabiliser, so to speak. It instantly became the chief ingredient of the offensive game.

It took twenty years for tennis to copy this stroke. The Swede Björn Borg was the first player who adopted topspin consistently with both forehand and backhand. And here's a great paradox, and of a historical nature to boot: a game born to mimic lawn tennis had suddenly revolutionised its nature and, in fact, become the inspiration for tennis. It was tennis, now, that was mimicking table tennis, but the result wasn't nearly as spectacular. The table tennis topspin is a far more devastating stroke than its tennis counterpart. The ball is much smaller and lighter, so a much higher number of rotations can be impressed on it with a well-executed spin – of any sort, not just topspin.

In 1977 the double-strung tennis racket was introduced, the so-called spaghetti racket. It was of normal size, but double-strung with ten main strings and five cross-strings. It could place thirty to sixty per cent more spin on the ball, and the spin was also unpredictable. As a table tennis player, this was music to my ears, but the United States Tennis Association argued that the racket would change the basic nature of the game – and banned it.

Tennis remains a sport that favours the players' physical stature and power. It missed its chance to evolve and become a more sophisticated game, unlike table tennis.

Indeed, table tennis had changed for ever. The two S's, Spin and Speed, had taken over. Gone was the Euclidean age of the hardbat, with very predictable trajectories and bounces – both on the table and off the racket – and never-ending rallies. Table tennis had become at once cerebral and snappy, something like a four-dimensional puzzle that one has to solve with no time to think about it.

The marriage between speed and spin was nothing short of alchemical. This may sound vague, but laboratories in Japan and China have been studying spin for the last few decades. In particular, they've been concentrating on the relative law of spin and speed.

A spinning ball in motion has a circumferential speed as well as a linear speed of the motion of its centre. These two speeds add up, and the ball may show the characteristics of *either* speed *if* it plays a leading role. When circumferential speed is higher than that of the ball centre, the trajectory is governed mainly by spin. When it is lower, it is speed that provides the main influence. And when the two speeds are approximately equal, the trajectory is influenced by both factors. *That* is the alchemical marriage of spin and speed, resulting in a ball that, as it accelerates on impact, may 'kick' up or 'dip' down, sometimes skipping to the side, too, if sidespin has been added to the stroke.

Both Japan and China are conducting theoretical research on spin that proceeds in conjunction with advances in science and technology. Equal attention is being paid to applied research, while quantitative research based on experimentation is being emphasised, too. Lastly, thorough investigations are being carried out with the aid of fluid mechanics, advanced mathematics, human biomechanics, artificial intelligence and material science. Not bad for a game that started as an after-dinner pastime played with books or cigar-box lids as rackets and with balls made out of cork!

But the honeymoon with spin brought about by the

foam-covered rackets risked being short-lived. In 1959–60 the ITTF – International Table Tennis Federation – banned the sponge racket, and standardised the thickness of a 'sandwich' composed of an ordinary pimpled rubber, whether or not inverted, and a thinner sponge. The sandwich was a compromise between the old hardbat and the new sponge racket.

As it turned out, the honeymoon was far from over. Sandwich rubbers were very effective in imparting spin too, and table tennis has not looked back since.

The sandwich revolution has turned the game into a highly sophisticated, non-Euclidean exercise. Much of the effort goes not only into returning the ball, but in *reading* exactly what kind of spin your opponent is about to hit, and how to counter it.

How difficult could this be? Apart from the serve, which is typically, but not necessarily, short, low and slow, everything else happens very fast: blink, and you'll have missed the ball. Then there are many types of spin. The basic four: topspin, backspin and sidespin in either direction. But, more accurately, there are eight: topspin combined with sidespin in either direction; backspin combined with sidespin in either direction; and an *infinite* number of combinations.

Imagine a ball coming towards you with backspin on it. It's flying in an almost straight line, and that is, with no parabolic curve, while it's spinning *backwards*. But your opponent has also placed *sidespin* on it, fading to your right. So the ball is also spinning *sideways*. In addition to those two spins, the ball may have retained some of the spin you yourself had imparted to it with your previous stroke. So, what kind of bounce will it produce on the table? And off your racket? The combination of different spins, speeds, angles and trajectories produces infinite variations, and in order to return the incoming ball properly, you must be constantly factoring in these four variables.

The small and very light ball is capable of rotating on three different axes perpendicular to one other, as well as in two directions on each of these axes. What can I say? The mystery deepens . . . It's a difficult concept to visualise, and even just reading it gives a good idea of the complexity of the ball's movements in the air. In addition to these natural properties of the ball, certain players who use very specific rubbers can make it fly in zigzag patterns.

One rarely used spin, mainly in serves, is the corkscrew spin. Paradoxically, advanced players can sometimes deceive one another with a 'no-spin' ball, by faking to be spinning and instead hitting a flat ball, which will prompt the deceived opponent to treat it as if it were spinning, and return the ball either long, wide or into the net. This may seem unnecessarily complicated, but remember the pace at which contemporary table tennis rallies are played, and keep in mind the mentioned factor of the alchemical marriage of spin with speed.

The sandwich revolution quickly brought about the king of all modern table tennis strokes: a codified form of topspin, the forehand loop. The whole body participates in the loop: the knees, first bent and then straightened;

the rotation of the waist; the backswing in preparation for the hit, to which the wrist also contributes; the transfer of the bodyweight from the right to the left foot; finally, after having hit the ball, the upward follow-through. The ball isn't just hit, but *brushed* upward with a very fast stroke. Thus an extremely heavy topspin is placed on it, which, owing to the Magnus effect, causes the ball to descend rapidly towards the opponent's side of the table. And, since when it touches it, it accelerates and kicks or dips, it's a devastating shot. Moreover, when the ball touches the opponent's racket, it tends to go up, thus making the return long. To counter this, the opponent has to 'close' his racket, by making it almost parallel to the table, depending on how much topspin it carries. But at times not even that is enough, so rather than trying to block, it's better to counter-topspin – which is easier said than done. World-class players do know how to handle incoming loops, and from time to time spectators are treated to a highly spectacular rally of loop drives.

No other sport relies so heavily on the Magnus effect, which is named after the German physicist Heinrich Magnus, who first described it in 1852. Larry Hodges, one of the leading experts on table tennis, explains it in the following layman terms:

Imagine a ball with topspin. As it travels through the air, the forward movement of the top of the ball forces air forward (or more precisely, slows down the movement of air over the top of the ball). This causes air to be 'clumped' together towards the front top of the ball, creating an area of high air density. Similarly, the backward movement of the bottom of the ball pulls air backward quickly, creating an area of low air density towards the front bottom of the ball. The high density air mass at the top of the ball forces the ball downward; the low density air mass at the bottom of the ball 'vacuums' it downward. The result: the ball drops. That's what makes a ball with topspin drop. The same applies to all spins, but as the spin orientation changes, the movement of the ball changes.

With the advent of the sandwich rubber, young players – in Asia, Europe and the Americas – adopted the topspin loop enthusiastically, while not-so-young players at first tried to oppose it but quickly faded away with their no longer effective hardbats. It was like the advent of gunpowder in warfare: arrows, spears, swords – all were phased out.

Spin – massive loads of it – is what determines the difference between the basement king and the advanced player. And although I'd never played in a basement, I realised that that was exactly where I belonged. In my blissful ignorance, I'd considered myself a good player all along; after all, hadn't the tournament on the cruise ship consecrated me as such? True, my son had sowed doubt, but in my delusions of TT prowess I'd come to put down his beating me to the hardbats that we'd played with, which could hardly produce any spin (my favourite weapon), or so I thought. And yet the Chinese players, by resorting to previously *unimaginable* amounts of spin on their every ball, had given me a reality check.

There was a classic tinge to this; it echoed what the ancient Greeks believed: that hubris would invariably be followed by nemesis. Indeed, hubris implies being out of touch with reality and overvaluing one's capabilities. Typically, my pride was followed by a sound punishment, inflicted upon me by the worshippers of the table tennis gods.

Humbling though it was, it didn't make me give up. I'm happy it didn't, because I was about to embark on a strange and, in many ways, awe-inspiring adventure. And should you happen to try this too, I hope you won't give up either, because the adventure is worth every minute of your time and every drop of your sweat.

Having savoured the true game in all its terrible beauty, I couldn't imagine leaving it at that. It was too astonishing. Yes, the beatings had been brutal and my inadequacy all too apparent. Would I ever learn to play as the advanced players did? I wasn't sure but, contrary to common sense, I wasn't repelled, but fascinated, enthralled. Looking clumsy and ridiculous in their eyes didn't matter to me, or rather, not enough to prevent me from going back. I'd give it another try and, if nothing else, witness the magic again. Who knows? Maybe, with a lot of effort, one day I myself would learn to produce some TT magic.

3
Initiation, War Tactics and Chinese Hurricanes

My transition from basement king to the lowliest subject at the court of the real kings of table tennis was nothing short of an initiation.

A proper initiation has little if anything to share with the contemporary practices of 'hazing' adopted by fraternities and the military and popularised in movies. In the last century the Romanian scholar Mircea Eliade defined three types of initiation rites: collective rites, including puberty initiations; secret rites, involving exclusive membership, and vocational rites with shamanic induction.

The first type of initiation still occurs in contemporary western societies, for example through Catholic Confirmation and Jewish Bar and Bat Mitzvah but, owing to the process of secularisation that we've undergone in the West, isn't as momentous as it used to be. The second type generally attracts bad press, as secret societies immediately come to mind that, under a thin veneer of 'initiatic' (the word of choice among initiates instead of 'initiatory') activities, have found a way to conceal themselves amid the fabric of society for the sake of power and illicit gain. The initiation I very unexpectedly underwent at the community centre was of the third type: vocational, in that no one had forced me to play table tennis and be humiliated by true experts, with hints of shamanic induction. And that is, if one of the very advanced players – which I felt were producing 'magic' – had found me to be at his level, he'd have welcomed me into the group as a fellow magician, or shaman.

While this seems extreme when related to a basement king who plays for the first time with advanced players, if the basement king is serious about table tennis (as I certainly was, otherwise I'd have remained underground, so to speak), his crushing defeats and ineptness will have a profound effect on him.

The overriding motif of initiation is the death of one's former self, and it represents a dying of childhood and an awakening to adulthood. Our very life 'initiates' with death and rebirth: as we struggle to be delivered from our mother's uterus, we feel that its contractions are strangling us. We're on the brink of suffocating, surely about to die. But once we're out, and breathing for the first time, we're in fact not only alive, but born, though if we had any recollection of our previous state, we should more correctly say *reborn*. Mimicking this, initiation affords the opportunity for rebirth as a new human being as both an individual rite of passage and a collective regeneration of the cosmos.

My table tennis initiation should have happened decades before. I wish that I had enrolled in a high-level tournament in my teens only to be eaten alive by every opponent. But that didn't happen, and besides, I might not have read anything into it other than the obvious fact that I was no good. The love for the game and the mysterious fascination with spin had stayed with me for all those years, but somehow I'd only been skimming the surface all along, never coming in contact with TT 'shamans.' All had changed in that community centre: there seemed to be no less than a shamanic convention there, and that evening I'd 'died' at their hand. Now it was time to be reborn, assuming or rather hoping that I'd learn the requisite technique and improve.

After initiation, the 'new life' doesn't come easily and demands full participation and alertness. Nothing brings this home more vividly than table tennis, which requires the fastest reflexes of any sport.

It comes as no surprise that in the contemporary world there should be a bias against initiation. The perception is that it reeks of elitism, but that's clearly not the case since, with the exception of C-section babies, we're *all* born the same way, and birth, or better the sudden transition from being a foetus to being a baby, is our first and most unrenounceable initiation. A traditional initiation is much more than a rite of passage that marks the entrance into a group; Eliade called it 'a basic change in one's existential condition.'

In the case of my TT initiation, my death had been obviously symbolic. Shocked and awed and crestfallen, I could have forgotten about *real* table tennis, said farewell to its 'shamans,' and continued, when the occasion arose, to be king among casual players. After all, in the kingdom of the blind the one-eyed man is king. And yet there was no denying the enormity of what I'd experienced. I couldn't turn my back to it, if nothing else out of wonder. It was time to be apprenticed, and hope for a real table tennis player to be born.

So I went back to the community centre and fumbled all over and around the table, chasing the ball frantically. Everyone there beat me regularly, even though I was now better equipped, by donning a more appropriate outfit and having bought, online, my first made-to-order racket. The shop would assemble it for me, so, with some help from their expert and pretending to know what I was talking about, I picked a certain rubber for the backhand, another type for the forehand, and the blade – three plies of wood, two of carbon – was of a different brand yet. I felt very geared up.

While the Cuban literatus – Emilio – was still defeating me, but at least not so easily, the various Chinese initiates kept walking all over me. Since I'm not a masochist, I sometimes wonder what made me go back for more. For one thing, unlike that kid in the summer camp in the Dolomites, the shamans were far less terrifying than those presiding over initiation in archaic cultures, except for the mute Iranian, who gave me surly looks and avoided me at all costs, making it eloquently known even without saying a word that I wasn't worthy of his time. The other shamans were mercifully not full of themselves, nor were they hostile, and would even praise, in their broken English, the few good shots I managed to produce.

Kai was particularly encouraging. Whether he was playing or waiting for his turn, he would exclaim: 'Good chop!', 'Good shot!', 'Good finish!' and, more often, 'Good D!' (which stands for 'defence'), as I'd be pushed far from the table trying hard to return loops and smashes.

Kai was between forty and fifty, not tall, a little chubby, and perennially smiling. Indeed, all the Chinese players smiled all the time. I realised then, and later in other clubs, that for the Chinese table tennis is a celebration, possibly even more so when they're overseas. They play with zest, enjoying themselves tremendously, and give every point their all. When I had to wait for my turn, I'd watch them keenly. The best ones were as quick as cats, with impressive coordination, highly spectacular in their attacks, and always looking for the put-away shot. Defence seemed to exist only as a state of emergency; nobody played defensively.

If sport is simulated war, then these Chinese players were surprisingly *not* following the teachings set down by their countryman, the Chinese general Sun Tzu, in his classic *The Art of War*, but rather those of the German-Prussian military theorist Carl von Clausewitz in *On War*. None of the former's 'Even though you are competent, appear to be incompetent,' but rather much of the latter's concentrated frontal attack.

Written over two thousand years ago by the mysterious warrior–philosopher, *The Art of War* remains one of the most influential treatises on strategy. Eagerly read by military leaders in the past, it's now studied by politicians and businessmen. Its aim is, as it should be, invincibility. But the way to accomplish it is refreshingly paradoxical: victory, if possible, without battle; strength through a thorough understanding of all the characteristics of conflict, be they physical, political or psychological. Some of Sun Tzu's teachings are baffling: 'All warfare is based on deception. Hence, when we are able to attack, we must seem unable; when using our forces, we must appear inactive; when we are near, we must make the enemy believe we are far away; when far away, we must make him believe we are near.' 'For to win one hundred victories in one hundred battles is not the acme of skill. To subdue the enemy without fighting is the acme of skill.'

At the opposite end of the spectrum there's *On War*, published posthumously in 1832. To say that von Clausewitz was Prussian rather than Chinese may suffice to describe his difference in mindset, but would be an oversimplification. His book has been of great consequence to the western world and beyond; among others, his concept of the 'fog of war' has made it clear that, even back in the early nineteenth century, war was far more complex and unpredictable than a game of chess. 'The great uncertainty of all data in war is a peculiar difficulty, because all action must, to a certain extent, be planned in a mere twilight, which in addition not infrequently – like the effect of a fog or moonshine – gives to things exaggerated dimensions and unnatural appearance.'

Still, *On War* isn't famed for its subtlety. 'War is an act of violence which in its application knows no bounds,' writes von Clausewitz. 'Kind-hearted people might of course think there was some ingenious way to disarm or defeat the enemy without too much bloodshed, and might imagine this is the true goal of the art of war. Pleasant as it sounds, it is a fallacy that must be exposed: war is such a dangerous business that the mistakes which come from kindness are the very worst.' 'If defence is the stronger form of war, yet has a negative object, it follows that it should be used only so long as weakness compels, and be abandoned as soon as we are strong enough to pursue a positive object.'

From the way the shamans of the community centre played, I could have sworn that they had eagerly read von Clausewitz rather that Sun Tzu. The latter is all about deception, secret agents, double agents, and so on. But, then, is deception possible in contemporary table tennis?

In my youth I used to deceive my sister with my primitive spins, but, like me, she was a beginner. Little deception seems possible at a high level, because one major difference between table tennis and war is that the former doesn't have what the military calls 'information uncertainty.'

Unlike a battle commander with incomplete intelligence about the opponent's weapons or troops, in a tournament the TT player routinely asks to inspect his opponent's racket before the match, and has learned to read all spins, or almost all. Occasionally a very advanced player may deceive his opponent with a no-spin ball, but the higher the level of play, the more unlikely this is to happen.

Once, both rubbers were allowed to be of the same colour – both red or both black – so that a player could have, for example, pips-out on one side, pips-in on the other, and switch sides even during a rally. That was certainly confusing for the opponent, but in 1986 the ITTF decreed that one rubber must be bright red and the other black, so that this sort of misinformation, or rather deception, would no longer be possible. The ITTF, in fact, seems bent on eliminating any sort of deception from the game. For example, it has further decreed that when one player is serving, the ball must be in the palm of the hand with which they don't hold the racket, in plain view, and tossed at least six inches up in the air before it's hit. Before this rule was introduced, clever (or tricky?) players were able to hide the ball behind themselves. With nothing short of a fast contortion, they'd strike it so that their movement would not be visible to the opponent, or only partially. This made it much more difficult to read the spin on the ball, which could only be guessed.

Because of this insistence on what the ITTF must in good faith perceive as fair play, most of the times the game is reduced to one essential: all-out frontal attack. Simple? Yes – and no: one of the typical paradoxes of table tennis. According to von Clausewitz, 'Everything in war is very simple. But the simplest thing is difficult.' Besides, the stern Prussian theorist can occasionally be as ambiguous as Sun Tzu, for example when he writes:

'Although our intellect always longs for clarity and certainty, our nature often finds uncertainty fascinating.'

Psychologically, I'd have preferred to be beaten by subtlety and deception rather than by swooshing loop–kills flying past me. That display of deadly power, spin and placement made me imagine how a duellist must have felt as he watched his opponent lunge at him unable to do anything to defend himself: he knew in advance that his sword would run him through, and so it would be. It was that brutal.

Then Kai taught me a great truth: 'I'm not a great player, and I don't improve, but I'm consistent.' I hope understatement is cultivated by the Chinese, because if Kai wasn't a great player then I was an abysmally bad one.

One thing that amused him very much was my being so self–disparaging. I'd try a certain stroke, the ball would go not where I intended it to go, by which I mean out or into the net, and I'd shout, '*Schifo!*' at the top of my lungs.

After a few times, Kai asked politely: 'Excuse me, what is "*schifo*"?'

'Italian for disgust, repulsion.'

Since then, if I made an obvious mistake out of clumsiness, Kai would say, '*Schifo!*' and smile like the Cheshire Cat. But he preferred to tell me, whenever possible, 'Good shot!', 'Good finish!', and so on.

Other Chinese players, among them a professor of physics and one of mathematics, both teaching at prestigious universities, were encouraging too, though they regularly allowed me 11–3, 11–4, or sometimes would be playing noticeably in slow motion, to give me a chance, which was even more humiliating because despite that I'd still lose. What could I learn from them, apart from everything?

I thought I'd start with their equipment. Most of them played with another mythical rubber, the Hurricane II, by Double Happiness. It couldn't be more aptly named. A hurricane develops tremendous circular wind motion that, when it touches land, results in widespread devastation. The faster the wind, the more 'spinny' its motion, the more havoc it wreaks.

Likewise, the Hurricane II rubber can impart tremendous spin to the ball so that, when it touches the table, it kicks and skips in a way that is devastating. The more powerful the player, the more spin they can impart, the more devastating the shot. As always when dealing with power, there's the issue of control: the more power, the less control. Hurricane II is a very powerful rubber, but also quite unforgiving; in order to control it, it demands of the player perfect movements. But I was blissfully unaware of this too, and decided that I'd equip myself with such a deadly weapon, without realising that there is also the original Hurricane rubber, as well as the yet more advanced Hurricane III.

Be it Hurricane I, II or III, the shamans had bought their rubbers in China and didn't know where to find them in the States. The online store from which I'd bought my racket publishes a thick catalogue. When reading the description of the rubbers they sold, I'd often come across 'Almost as tacky [which in TT jargon means 'sticky'] as a Chinese rubber.' But why should I be content with 'almost'? I wanted the total immersion, the full-impact experience of the sticky and hard Chinese rubbers. Why couldn't they sell a Chinese rubber directly?

I called them up and asked. 'We'd love to, but the quality is so erratic – we just can't do that to our clients.'

Erratic quality? How could that be? Is that why most of the best players in the world are Chinese and use mainly Chinese equipment? It didn't make sense, and I found out later that, while a high-quality Japanese or European rubber costs at least fifty dollars, but often more, an equally good Chinese one, if with different characteristics, costs around twenty, or a little more, but even much less.

I quickly decided never to buy Japanese or European equipment again (as for Korean, I didn't realise it existed), but to go exclusively Chinese. It goes without saying that this was an irrational decision, since how could I know what was really suitable for me, and how could I rule out hundreds of excellent European and Japanese rubbers without ever trying them? Still, Chinese players were my early model, and it seemed natural that I'd use their stuff. Besides, hadn't Sun Tzu written, 'If you know both yourself and your enemy, you can win a hundred battles without a single loss'? I could start to know my enemy by possessing myself of his weapons.

I finally found an online store based in California that specialises in Chinese brands for 'table tennis, badminton, Taichi and Wushu,' and bought myself a couple of made-to-order rackets.

When they arrived in the mail, I'm not embarrassed to say that it felt like a childhood Christmas. The rubbers were almost as sticky as Scotch tape. I was in awe of these little wonders, and felt instantly empowered. I thought I'd test them first on Emilio.

He had a table in the basement of his home. I'd go there, he'd offer me Martinelli's non-alcoholic sparkling cider, and we'd play with Cuban music blasting all out. And guess what? With my brand-new Chinese equipment I was playing . . . worse.

What an unforgiving game. There's no shortcut, is there? I'd think as I tried to cope with his strokes, which he imparted effortlessly following the rhythm of a mambo.

I was still losing most of my games, despite my goodwill and my Chinese Hurricane rubbers, but I had made a friend. Emilio and I would chat about literature, Cuba, and he about women, his favourite subject. Having learned Spanish in Miami in order to survive in a city in which English is only occasionally spoken, I have a weak spot for Cubans in the US. Despite having been forced into exile, and despite a life of more than ordinary struggle, they've prospered while miraculously preserving their sense of humour. Emilio is no exception. He drives a vintage Mercedes convertible, plays table tennis *and* tennis, dates several women simultaneously with a concept of loyalty all his own, and speaks four languages fluently, in addition to being very well read. And he's written a not-too-flattering novel about the Kennedys since, like every Cuban exile, he's obsessed with them.

It's perhaps thanks to Emilio and to his nonchalant approach to life that I took my slow progress in TT with a grain of salt. I wasn't going to abort my initiation; also because the shamans were patient and, graciously, allowed me to take my time. I watched the advanced players keenly, when they played me and when I observed them as I waited for my turn. I tried to imitate their motions, was now playing with their equipment, but progress was slow. Was I just not cut out for TT after all? I'd always liked it and now that I had chanced on the real game I was also awed and mesmerised by it. But maybe I should be happy just to be a spectator. How could a man pushing eighty still beat me? It's true that Emilio was no newcomer to the game and had accumulated a number of gold medals competing in tournaments for men of his age. But still . . .

From time to time, I'd reread passages from *The Art of War*. The following seemed spot on: 'Anger may in time change to gladness; vexation may be succeeded by content.'

I didn't give up, but kept playing, trying to develop a certain finesse of the hand, rather than power, my emphasis being always on spin. And then, after five or six months, it happened.

I finally began to make some sense out of the myriad shots that the Chinese and everyone else threw at me. I memorised the motions they made – with the hand *and* the elbow, without realising yet that I should have been watching for the movement of the whole body – as they hit the ball – and especially how the ball bounced on the table. Things began to fall into place, and I had my first few wins.

Kai was impressed. Not that I beat him – far from it – but sometimes I pulled out of my hat some impossible shot that did land on his side of the table. He'd look at me astonished and say: 'Very good finish!' and ask where it came from. What he took for a masterstroke was, in fact, an unnecessary risk, a *bel gesto*, a fancy gesture, that Italian curse that often makes an Italian opt for the difficult, almost impossible shot rather than for the more reliable but less fanciful alternative. But at least I had the audacity to try it, and sometimes it worked. This wasn't the right approach at all, and in time I'd have to *unlearn* it, but it still carried me across the great divide between being a non-player and, at last, an apprentice.

As for Emilio, I now beat him consistently, wondering how it'd been possible, previously, for him to beat *me* so easily. The time allotted at the community centre was only two hours three times a week. I knew that I was improving at last, but needed more time to practise. One of the shamans one day mentioned a club with long playing hours five times a week. Further away, in Arlington, but, I thought, worth a try.

4

The Humbleness of Giants, and the Lingua Franca of Table Tennis

The new place was a proper club, with a membership fee and four tables in as many rooms. It operated with a more forgiving rule: each player gets to play two matches, whether he wins or loses, and then leaves his space to the next person waiting. This was conspicuously anti-initiatic, and I must say it felt wonderful. How's a player to improve if every time they lose a match they're sent back to the end of the line? By being allowed to play more, the not-so-good player stands a chance to learn something other than humbleness, on which I was by now an expert.

My first time there was a busy evening. I watched a furious match between a passionate Russian and a cool African American, followed by one between the Russian, who was still on, and an Egyptian whom we'll meet again, who immediately struck me as being full of himself and yet at the same time possessing an awkward style; then a Filipino; then a man with a charming southern drawl. He was from Alabama, as it turned out, and Tom is the epitome of the southern gentleman. When I stepped up to the table he greeted me courteously and briefly explained the club's rules. Even as we warmed up I could tell that he had better control than I had. The confirmation came with the match: I lost 11–3, 11–4 to a man in his sixties with a good fore-hand *and* backhand loop and a decidedly aggressive approach. When we were done, he said, 'I enjoyed that,' looking as if he meant it. We shook hands and he stepped aside. Thanks to the club's forgiving rule I was still up, though my instinct was to leave the table, since I'd been defeated. I knew that everybody in the room was thinking what I myself was, that I was not very good. But Tom had offered his white lie convincingly.

Another man welcoming newcomers was Joe, short and with a very fit, muscular physique. He was wearing safety goggles, and explained to me why.

Through a series of unfortunate circumstances twelve years before, Joe had lost the use of his right eye. His remaining eye was so precious that he felt more protected against incoming balls by the goggles. A lawyer by profession, he'd always loved table tennis. Indeed, in the Seventies he had travelled to Sweden especially to 'check out the TT scene there' and buy some equipment, including a Stiga net, which he still has and which, remarkably, is still usable. The sudden loss of vision from his right eye had thrown him into a state of despair, but not for long. He has a sunny disposition, as I found out, and refused to be defeated. He trained himself to see and function using a single eye. The one thing he missed the most, though, was table tennis.

'Eventually,' he told me as we were warming up, 'I went to my old club and tried my hand at it. I didn't care if I made a fool of myself, I just couldn't live without table tennis any more.'

'And it went well, right?' I asked, judging by his clean strokes.

'No, not that well at first. I've since become an expert on vision. The mental processes at work of a person who sees with two eyes is called "binocular stereopsis." It enables the brain to perceive certain additional depth in the form of a mental construct. Close one eye, and you shut down this stereo construct. My depth perception sucks. I've had to train myself to *imagine* it. I've had to adapt my style, and still miss or mis-hit balls, especially on my blind side, that I'd never have missed.' He picked up the ball from the floor and added, 'And there's more: with my "good" eye I see double and have blind spots.'

'I'm very sorry to hear that.'

'That's all right, play as you normally would, don't change anything for me,' he said.

Still, I decided to take it easy on him. But no need for that: his serves alone were as insidious as they get, beyond my control back then, and I returned many of them wide, or into the net. And his other shots were just as good. In short, he beat me soundly, and since then I've always played to the best of my ability with him. He had a lot about table tennis to teach, and even more about life.

And what to say of the passionate Russian, Alex, one of the first players I met there? Somewhat overweight, he sweated profusely, cursed in Russian, and exulted loudly when his lightning-fast forehand loop drive scored a point. As a young man in the Soviet Union he had trained as a boxer and knew that when throwing a punch the whole body throws it, not just the arm – much as how in table tennis a loop is powered by your entire body, culminating with a snap of the wrist for a final bit of added oomph. Only in his early forties, he had already had an eventful life.

Alex had been sent to Siberia to 'work as a slave' during the two-year-long compulsory military service. If laying railway tracks over frozen ground was not bad enough, he was constantly picked on for being both a Muscovite and a Jew (he had 'Jew' stamped on his passport). Being picked on by Soviet soldiers meant, he eventually told me, being cornered – outnumbered – when no officers were around, and pummelled. Once back in Moscow, he decided to emigrate to Israel. He didn't speak a word of Hebrew, but learned it there along with English while he worked *and* participated in the reserve service, a military service in which citizens are summoned for active duty of at most a month every year.

A graduate of Lomonosov Moscow State University, he finally came to the US to work as an information technology wizard. Given his troubled past, behaviourist psychology would diagnose him as a candidate for a maladapted life, an individual likely to develop chronic stress, if not a possible sociopath. So much for facile determinism: if that were the case then most of the world's population would be made up of maladapted sociopaths, since it's a sad reality that many children in developing countries grow up in underprivileged conditions, if not in outright misery.

Indeed, a difficult life has *not* hardened Alex's heart. Whenever he plays with a female member of the club, being a big and strong man he holds back on power, and never smashes, so that, in the end, he loses, but with a smile on his face. Nor does he swear in the presence of women. There's such decency and dignity about this benevolent Russian bear. Recently, on hearing that I had a significant wedding anniversary coming up, he arrived at the club with a gift: a bottle of special vodka.

Gilbert, the Filipino player, despite the handicap of a permanent limp due to having damaged one of his knees in an accident, had two physically demanding jobs: delivering papers in the very early morning, and then as the handyman in charge of a large apartment complex. Sometimes, as he waited for his turn to play sitting on a chair, he would doze off from over-exhaustion. In spite of that, not only was he always pleasant, including with newcomers such as myself who certainly didn't offer an exciting level of play, but he helped the less skilful players improve their game. He'd routinely set up a ball collector at one end of the table and, standing on one side, serve ball after ball to the player he was coaching, often a total or near stranger, until he or she perfected whichever stroke they were working on. All of this for free and with a cheerful disposition from a man who had barely enough energy to stay awake.

One day an old man showed up, short and with big ears. I was immediately struck by something almost beatific in his expression. Hien was a good player, too. As we warmed up, he apologised for not being in top shape. 'I used to play in my youth, in Vietnam,' he explained. 'But then the war came, and I was captured. I spent eight years in prison.'

'That's terrible,' I said. 'I'm very sorry for you.' I felt stupid as I said this: words seemed inadequate.

'The first year,' he resumed, smiling, 'was the best one – no torture!' He didn't elaborate – didn't seem to care to. He only added, 'But that's water under the bridge now,' and concentrated on his strokes.

Hien played with the enthusiasm and delight of a child. Once more I was standing in front of a man who had overcome incredible obstacles and, miraculously, kept his sanity. More than that: there was something about him so serene that it bordered on the saintly.

We've all heard of post-traumatic stress disorder, or PTSD, which has been popularised by films about the Vietnam War and the effect it had on veterans coming home. In my small way, I experienced that mix of anxiety, insomnia, claustrophobia and dread after a horrific car accident in which the people in the car that hit mine died, and I, after surgery, was confined to a bed for three months. It took yet more surgery and a long time for the bones to heal, but longer for the psyche.

Meeting Joe, Alex, Gilbert and Hien reminded of those dark days after my accident. And yet Joe, after losing his right eye and sharpness of vision in his left one, could not afford to have PTSD: he had a wife, three kids to put through college, and was the main source of income. Despite his greatly diminished vision, he managed to continue to work. Alex had to put the Soviet Union, his family and the life he'd known there behind him and, alone in Israel, had learned two languages while quickly finding employment. He too couldn't afford to have PTSD. Gilbert had left in the Philippines a history of hardships in search of a better future, and had a wife, and then a little daughter, to take care of. He had barely enough time to sleep, let alone worry about PTSD. And Hien eventually succeeded in coming to the States: all he had were the clothes he was wearing.

How did I feel, then, next to these giants? Dwarfed, and still do. Whether I win or lose when we play, I realise that it's an honour just to be in their company. But what was it about table tennis? How come such a seemingly airy and light game attracted such strong souls, such giants of the human spirit?

I eventually understood: humbleness, humility. The four giants had been humiliated, either by ill fortune or by sadistic persecutors. But, miraculously, they had survived their ordeals, without losing any of their decency and dignity. None of them would approve of my writing about them in such glowing terms. In fact, they'd hate it.

Both 'humility' and 'humbleness' come from 'humus,' the dark organic material in soils. The word 'human' comes from humus, too. It's only the greatest among us humans who know extreme humility. Golda Meir, the Iron Lady of Israeli politics, once said: 'Don't be so humble; you're not that great.' It seems to me that people who possess humility to such an extent are, really, superhuman.

Table tennis, as I'd been discovering, is a humbling discipline. But the four giants had no false pride and were patient with themselves and with everyone around them. I'm tempted to say that all four, irrespective of their nationality and background, seemed to embody the three jewels of the Tao: compassion, moderation and humility. If the intended result of Taoism is striking a balance with the universe, or its source, and that is, the Tao, then Joe, Alex, Gilbert and Hien had got closer to it than anyone I'd ever met. That they should be such fans of table tennis is a testament to its depths.

I'd become a member of the club, and begun to study the strokes of the best players. These were from all over the world. Some of them refugees, others eccentrics, rarely jocks; all with interesting stories to tell. I'll never forget an Afghan refugee recently arrived in the US; after a few matches, he was thirsty, so I directed him to the drinking fountain in the hallway and showed him how to operate it. After he drank, there were tears in his eyes: never in his life had he taken water for granted, let alone that it would be potable.

I've since realised that there exists a supranational tribe that numbers close to four hundred million and goes under the name of The United Colours of Table Tennis. Were it not for TT, how often would you interact, as I have, with someone from Madagascar? Or Mongolia? Or Suriname? Or Kyrgyzstan – and where is that, exactly? And, even when I meet with a player for the first time, with the kind of familiarity that is ever a surprise? The language barrier is eliminated, as we all speak the lingua franca of TT. In fact, as in time I began to frequent clubs all around the country, I came to the realisation that *every* barrier is eliminated: class, colour, race, creed, and so on. The TT planet seems to be a parallel world, de facto more enlightened, fair and friendly than the one we normally live in.

5

Lost in Translation, and Prophecies

At the club I began to experiment with a wide variety of players, and at the same time freed myself from the constraints of having to order a racket always from the same place so that they'd assemble it for me. I armed myself with a precision knife, glue and patience. Gluing a rubber onto the blade and then cutting it to the exact size is not astrophysics, but is not especially easy either. It took a number of attempts to do it well, and then I hit the Web with a vengeance. In the globalised world of the most cosmopolitan sport of them all, I bought rubbers from China, Taiwan, Malaysia, Australia, Canada and . . . Oregon and California. Always Chinese rubbers, but wherever I could find them cheaper, of the provincial or national type used by professional Chinese players.

It was a period of experimentation as exhilarating as it was disorienting. Rubbers are classified according to their speed, spin, control, sponge thickness and hardness.

Weight is another factor, and then there is the 'tackiness' if they're sticky, and the 'grip' if they aren't, as well as the arc, low or high, of the loop, if specified. Lastly, their reaction to the incoming ball is classified as 'high-throw' or 'low-throw'. All this is confusing enough for the novice, but then there's something beyond confusing and outright 'sibylline.'

The ageless Cumean Sibyl – the priestess presiding over the Apollonian Oracle at Cumae, a Greek colony near Naples, Italy – prophesied by singing the fates and then writing on oak leaves. Such leaves were arranged inside the entrance of her cave, but if the wind scattered them (and – wouldn't you know it? – it was *always* windy) she wouldn't help to reassemble them in the original order. Therefore the people asking for the prophecy would be, to say the least, baffled, unable to piece together the puzzle in a coherent way.

Without realising it, most Chinese table tennis manu-facturers behave similarly by feeding the descriptions of their products to nonhuman Web translators, and much is lost in translation, to the point that the descriptions become oracles, and positively cryptic ones at that: 'Colloid combined with flexibility and glutinosity perfectly, the act extent of loop is becoming small and piercing;' 'More tender, strain and long-time stickiness under the wonderful function of molecule;' 'She has exquisite technology and acute beat feeling,' a few of many examples of 'Chinglish.'

As China has opened up to the rest of the world only recently, English isn't yet widely known or understood.

But since the Web offers many nonhuman translation possibilities, why not exploit them? The country abounds with mistranslations: 'Man and wife lung slice,' a restaurant proudly advertises; another one: 'Orange juice, lemon juice, strange juice;' the advertisement for Fuji condoms enticingly proclaims 'DAMAGE;' a bank's ATM attracts customers by letting them know that it is a 'cash recycling machine;' an art supplies store states, invitingly, 'Free yourself from the misery of existence,' thinking it an artistic name; 'Your careful step keeps tiny grass invariably green;' 'Pepsi brings your ancestors back from the grave;' 'Garden with curled poo;' 'I like your smile but unlike you put your shoes on my face;' 'Please keep chair in position & keep table cleaned after dying. Thanks for your corporation.' The examples are countless; the whole country is a lost-in-translation festival.

Table tennis manufacturers have joined the party with gusto, their products' descriptions being as cryptic as it gets. It's fitting that these would be Chinese rubbers, and that the whole country should be producing so many sibylline statements, thousands upon thousands of them. It reminds me of the Chinese classic I Ching, or Book of Changes, which, if for completely different reasons, gives equally puzzling oracles.

This book is both a marvel and a mystery. The analytical psychologist Edward Whitmont described it as 'a collection of situational images and judgements reflecting the varieties of the human condition in their relation to self and cosmos.' It's centred on the Taoist dynamic balance of the opposites Yin (the dark negative feminine principle) and Yang (the bright positive masculine principle). The I Ching further hinges on the evolution of events as a process, and the acceptance of the inevitability of change to which one can be better prepared by consulting the book.

Without going into great detail, it's useful to explain that the text of the I Ching is a very thorough collection of oracular statements represented by sixty-four sets of six lines each: the hexagrams. Each of the hexagrams' six horizontal lines is either Yang (an *unbroken* or *solid* line), or Yin (*broken*, an *open* line with a gap in the centre). With six such lines stacked from bottom to top there are the sixty-four possible combinations. Scholars have traditionally considered it a philosophical and cosmological book, but it has also been used extensively as a divination system to predict the future. How?

To use the I Ching as an oracle, one asks a specific question and then randomly gathers bundles of sticks or, more expediently, tosses three coins. The numerical patterns cast with either method correspond to a hexagram in the book, to which in turn correspond images and judgements. This can be an unchanging hexagram, or it can have changing lines, which need to be identified by following a simple procedure. Such lines are additional angles to the hexagram, and sometimes may even seem to contradict it. They may point to choices and opportunities, or dangers and pitfalls, and provide useful advice on how to deal with them appropriately. This part of the reading is the most specific to the present situation. In sum, both the primary hexagram and its changing lines must be interpreted as answers to the question asked. And here comes the difficult part, as the interpretation of the I Ching oracles is an art in itself.

For example, Hexagram 42. I / Increase. The trigram above is SUN, The Gentle, Wind; the trigram below, CHÊN, The Arousing, Thunder. In the sinologist Richard Wilhelm's groundbreaking translation:

> The idea of increase is expressed in the fact that the strong lowest line of the upper trigram has sunk down and taken its place under the lower trigram. This conception also expresses the fundamental idea on which the Book of Changes is based. To rule truly is to serve. A sacrifice of the higher element that produces an increase of the lower is called an out-and-out increase: it indicates the spirit that alone has power to help the world.

The Judgement: It furthers one / To undertake something. / It furthers one to cross the great water.'

This seems straightforward enough, but in fact its explanation has no lack of contradictory nuances that are difficult to assimilate for a western mind. And then there may be the changing lines, which add more information. Other hexagrams are more difficult to interpret, such as 46. Shêng / Pushing Upward. Above: K'UN, The Receptive, Earth; below: SUN, The Gentle, Wind, Wood. The Judgement: Pushing Upward has supreme success. / One must see the great man. / Fear not. / Departure toward the south / Brings good fortune.

C. G. Jung, the influential thinker and founder of

analytical psychology, was the first to divulge this extra-ordinary oracular book in the West, through the transla-tion of the quoted Richard Wilhelm. Jung and many Jungian psychologists swear to the accuracy of the predic-tions – or better, prophecies – the oracle is capable of when consulted with the proper approach.

I myself have consulted it many times in my life. In fact, my wife, who's become adept at reading the cast coins, used to keep a diary in which she listed in chronological order the questions I asked and the oracles I received in response. I hadn't consulted the I Ching in a long time, though, until table tennis brought it back to the fore through the cryptic descriptions about the Chinese rubbers, as well as through the strange thoughts expressed from time to time by Chinese players in my presence. I was never sure if the ambiguity of what they said was due to their tentative English, to their mindset, so different from ours, or to both, or neither. It was *that* puzzling.

Nowadays one can cast the coins virtually, online, clicking on the mouse six times, though I wonder if that is a valid method? Anyway, the question is: does the Book of Changes work? Does it provide accurate predictions?

The reply is composite. Also because, as the sceptics would maintain, if you want to be in the oracular business for a long time, you had better keep your oracles vague and ambiguous, and yet at the same time not completely absurd. That is a talent in its own right. There's a precedent in our western tradition.

The Delphic Oracle was established on the slopes of

Mount Parnassus, in Greece, in the eighth century BC; its last recorded response was given in AD 393, and only because Emperor Theodosius I ordered pagan temples to shut down. For more than a millennium, the Delphic Oracle was the most authoritative oracle not only in Greece but arguably in the whole western world. The priestess of the temple was the Pythia, whose prophecies were inspired directly by the god Apollo.

In an overwhelmingly patriarchal society, the Pythia was the one exception, a woman who wielded immense power, as all sorts of dignitaries and heads of state came to the temple to consult her. Historians today are in agreement that the Pythia delivered oracles in a frenzied state possibly induced by mind-altering vapours rising from a chasm in the rock, and that the attending priests reshaped the gibberish that she spoke into enigmatic prophecies. How else, the sceptics would chime in, could such rank nonsense perpetuate itself for well over a millennium with impunity? If the oracles had been unambiguous and to the point, it would have been only too easy to verify their accuracy, or lack thereof. The realisation might have soon dawned that the entire operation was a fraud. But was it? To remain operative for so long seems to imply that many must have thought that the prophecies were, if not exactly accurate, at least useful.

When it comes to the I Ching, Chinese philosophers frown on the idea of trivialising it by using it as an oracle. It's not a fortune-telling gimmick, and in fact the book itself seems to resent and frustrate those who consult it to learn about their future (there's nothing like trying to consult it periodically to realise this empirically). What the I Ching seems to have done best for the last five thousand years – first as it was passed on orally, and then since it was written down in a book – is to take an individual beyond the limits of his or her vision and senses so as to describe one's situation as it is at present with its latent possibilities. Jung wrote: 'The Chinese mentality, as I see it at work in the I Ching, seems to be exclusively preoccupied with the accidental aspects of events. What we call coincidence seems to be the main thing this peculiar mentality is interested in, whereas what we highly regard as causality goes almost unnoticed.'

Causality, the relation between cause and effect, is one of the building blocks of western culture – and one of its most effective jailers. For our western mindset based on verifiable causal phenomena it takes a leap of faith to accept the idea that by throwing three coins in the air six times in a row we cast a hexagram whose 'vignette' and changing lines, if any, represent exactly where we stand at this precise point in time and what potentialities – or setbacks – lie ahead of us if we proceed on a certain course.

A new entry to our club, a lanky, head-in-the-clouds Chinese man in his fifties who looked thirty-something at most, must be introduced here, as he shed light on this crucial difference between East and West, and that is, accidentality versus causality. The first time I saw him, we played a bit, and he said hardly a word. Eventually I asked his name.

'Harbin.'

'Did you say "Harbin"? Isn't that a city in Northern China?'

'Yes, they named it after me.' The delivery was so deadpan, for a short while he had us all fooled, making us believe that he'd given his name to a city over four thousand years old and now of ten million inhabitants. The trickster had arrived.

In the months to come I witnessed the oddest behaviour from Harbin and, once he felt at home at the club, heard the strangest remarks. He had an understanding of luck that kept coming up during our hard-fought matches.

For us western players, a lucky shot is one that hits the net, or the edge or, luckier yet, both net *and* edge; or one that hits your finger but still manages to get across the net, or the edge of your racket. I've never seen a player inadvertently hit the ball with their finger and the ball then going on to hit the net *and* the edge, but conceivably it could happen. In other words, a lucky shot is one in which there's an *accidental intervention*, an *unforeseen element of chance*. But if a western player deliberately chooses to execute a particularly technically demanding shot, and if that shot does land on the table, in his view it has nothing to do with luck, but everything to do with skill. For Chinese players, on the other hand, the concepts of 'lucky' and 'deliberate' aren't mutually exclusive. In their view, a technically demanding but deliberate shot that works is, in fact, a lucky shot. It's a high-risk shot that paid off, and luck had its part in it. So it seems that for a Chinese mindset accidentality and causality are still interrelated, precisely as described by the I Ching.

The more I thought about the I Ching in relation to

table tennis, the more obvious it seemed why not only the Chinese but East Asians as a whole should be such supremely skilful players. How could the mastering of the balance between Yin and Yang not play a direct role in the performance of a TT champion, or a martial artist, for that matter?

In the western world we're still getting lost in our chasing after cause and effect, making plans accordingly, and quickly coming up with plan B, and then even C when also the back-up plan goes awry. It's a never-ending titanic struggle against the imponderability of life and is, all things considered, a lost cause. Even here in the West any very successful man or woman when asked about the secret behind their success, will reply that in addition to hard work and perseverance luck played a relevant role. But luck in the western world is still perceived as random chance. Fortuna, the Roman goddess of chance, was portrayed as being blindfolded. And Fortuna is no remote concept, but lives on in our words 'fortune,' 'fortune-teller,' 'fortunate' and 'unfortunate.' The I Ching may be able to show us westerners that Fortuna, rather than being blindfolded, can, in fact, *see*.

The twentieth-century philosopher and mathematician Alfred North Whitehead wrote, 'Life is an offensive, directed against the repetitious mechanism of the Universe.' The I Ching can help the superior man or woman to be in step with such a mechanism so that, out of the general assembly of potentialities, he or she chooses, in Whitehead's words, 'that which undergoes the formality of actually occurring.' It points to that window of opportunity, that change through which one has somewhere between zip and, say, a thousand to come to terms with, and improve on, the mystery of being.

I still experiment with the I Ching, much as I experiment with Chinese rubbers from across the Pacific. Down the years, time and again I've cast oracles containing the promising phrase, 'It furthers one to cross the great water.' I realise that it's a pronouncement open to various interpretations according to the hexagram it is found in, but every time I read 'the great water,' I think of the Earth's largest ocean, the Pacific. To me, 'crossing the great water' has always meant heading towards the Far East by crossing the Pacific – a prophecy that, in time, came true.

6
Finding Your Way –
The Importance
of the Teacher

I was improving, but not exactly in a hurry. In a book by Plato I'd come across a passage that had become my mantra: 'Never discourage anyone . . . who continually makes progress, no matter how slow.'

With the Internet and enthusiasm as heady accomplices, I amassed a collection of blades, seven of them. The blade's wood can be combined with materials of different properties to enhance the playing performance. Often blades feature one or more carbon layers within them to boost their speed. Other materials include titanium, fibreglass, cork and the mysterious acrylate and aramids (might they come from meteorites? Apparently not: acrylates are the salt and esters of acrylic acid while aramids are a class of synthetic fibres). A few of my blades were made of five plies of pure wood. No one had told me that these still offer the best control and touch, but I would eventually realise it. And then there was the 'sweet spot,' which sounded very nice but, as it turned out, doesn't mean honey-coated.

The sweet spot is the most solid area in the centre of the blade. In cheaper blades, the ball doesn't bounce off its outside edges as well as it does off its centre. But blades of a higher quality offer larger sweet spots, so that the player doesn't need to concentrate on hitting the ball always in the dead centre of his racket.

I collected even more rubbers, all inexpensive as they were Chinese. It seemed the obvious choice, but the Chinese rubbers' advantage of being cheaper than the Japanese, Korean and European ones was upset by the disadvantage of being more demanding of the player's skills. Without realising it, therefore, I was complicating my learning process by equipping myself with rubbers – and blades – beyond my level. To add to the confusion, I kept changing combinations, peeling rubbers from one blade and gluing them onto another.

Then there was speed glue, nothing less than an obsession among advanced players, who remove the rubber from the blade and re-glue it before playing. Within twenty to thirty minutes, the glue expands the sponge, thus adding extra speed and spin to the rubber, and the effect lasts for a few hours.

I remember a rubber in particular for its effect on my opponents, one whose name ought to be preceded by a drum roll: the Kokutaku Blütenkirsche 868 Tokyo Super Tacky Japanese Style. Before starting a match, I'd announce: 'Beware, on my backhand I've got a . . . Kokutaku Blütenkirsche! You've been warned.'

'A *what*?' they'd ask.

'A Kokutaku Blütenkirsche! Watch out!'

And wouldn't you know it? During the first rallies they'd play poorly, expecting Heaven knows what from my backhand strokes.

Isn't that rubber a mouthful? I'd bought it over the Web and it had come all the way from Hong Kong. It was a curious hybrid between Chinese and Japanese; Kokutaku is the brand; Blütenkirsche the specific rubber. I later discovered that Blütenkirsche means – in German – 'flowering cherry tree,' and refers to the common Japanese flowering cherry. It's a nice way to confuse things, with a hard-to-pronounce mouthful in multiple languages. For the extremely modest price, the rubber was quite good, if not exceptionally good. But there was nothing like saying its name out loud to send shivers down the spine of my unknowing opponents: 'Kokutaku Blütenkirsche!'

Unleashing me among endless combinations of blades, rubbers and speed glues was like setting a child loose in a candy store: the least that would happen would be indigestion. And indigestion did happen.

For one thing, in my quest for the perfect combo I didn't realise that I was making it effectively impossible for the muscle memory related to my strokes to form through repetition. This process decreases the need for concentration on the movement required by the specific stroke, and also brings about maximum efficiency within the motor and memory systems. But different rubbers, blades and speed glues react very differently from one another, and all require constant adjustment. As a result, I was always playing tentatively.

In time, I began to favour a certain combo and play mostly with it, and gave up speed glue altogether. I was not one of them, but I began to suspect that top players were all closet glue sniffers. Voluntary or involuntary, they were all sniffers so, to avoid a health hazard, the ITTF has recently banned the use of speed glue. Moreover, the fastest blades, with carbon plies among the wooden ones, and the fastest rubbers with the thickest sponges weren't necessarily my best allies. The more power is available, the more control it takes to master them. In table tennis, as in anything, control is essential and, at that stage, I didn't have much of it.

The more I played, the more I got over my initial equipment orgy, donating rackets to club members and refusing to buy any fancy accessories. I wore a cheap pair of canvas sneakers, whose lightness, however, was ideal for the footwork required. A black cotton polo with cotton shorts, no artificial fabrics with all the colours of a clown costume and big logos. To complete my outfit, a replica of those olive-green cloth bags used in China during the Cultural Revolution, with a big red star on its front and written in Mandarin: 'Serve for the people.'

Because I apply to my racket's rubbers what a female member of the club thinks is a 'lotion,' she calls me a metrosexual. In fact, the 'lotion' is Spinmax, which keeps the rubbers tacky indefinitely. On the other hand, all

Chinese players marvel at my bag, as nowadays many Chinese people seem to lean more towards Gucci bags.

The club attracted players of all ages. The middle-agers had one thing in common: problems with some part of their body, usually as a result of being too athletic in their youth, as they would explain. The knee in particular seemed to be the first joint to give up, be it the cartilage, the cruciate ligaments, the menisci or the whole knee. Many players of a certain age played with knee braces, some with elbow or wrist braces, too. The Roman poet Juvenal is responsible for the famous statement, '*Mens sana in corpore sano*' (a sound mind in a sound body). In my brainy youth I was aware of such words of wisdom, but critical of them. So, I had diligently steered clear of jocks and all sorts of athletic overexertion, and here I was: despite my many fractures, ironically in better shape than many of these former jocks.

I've since begun to suspect that sport becomes useful and indeed necessary once you are past forty. That's when the body needs to be kept in shape to fight off the tendency to put on weight and its attendant dangers: high cholesterol, high blood pressure, high blood sugar levels, and so on. Before that, young men and women, in a recurring rapture of physical exuberance, can tend to overdo it, and will pay for that later on in their life.

I was now known at the club as the 'spin master,' one who induced headaches in less cerebral players, as I had been exploring my original passion. Even with a compact stroke, the tacky Chinese rubbers produced tremendous friction, imparting very heavy spin. A Chinese woman would don a smile whenever she saw me. When we played, and with shot after shot I'd spin increasingly more, she'd gape in awe and eventually burst into an ecstatic, 'Oh, what spin, what spin – you're the spin doctor!' with a tone that reminded me of Teri Garr as the laboratory assistant in the film *Young Frankenstein* when she utters, admiringly: 'Oh, Doctor!'

Some club members were flat hitters: players who simply smack the ball as powerfully as they can. My backspinned chops broke their game, as they would return them into the net time after time. Of course, the better players, and most Asian players, knew just how to lift the ball, and then *I* was in trouble.

One day I was waiting my turn to play with an Austrian gearhead. He was dressed from head to toe in Joola gear, an excellent but very expensive German manufacturer. His racket was Joola, too, top of the line, and so were his shoes. He was wearing close to a thousand dollars in gear, which, for table tennis, is extravagant. From the way he played and moved about, one could tell that he felt very confident about himself. My turn came; we'd never played one another. During the warm-up, I gave him none of my spins, just pushed the ball flatly across the net. Then, under the eyes of a member I'd never met, the match began.

I felt inspired to give the gearhead my whole repertoire of serves. Returning them gave him hell: most he landed into the net; others were long; others yet wide. In the end, he couldn't return a single one. I was enjoying myself tremendously but kept a straight face.

When *he* served, I would spin the ball back in a way

that left him dumbfounded. I won the first game by a very wide margin.

The member I'd never met had been commenting all along, speaking in Spanish to a young Frenchman I knew. 'Very clever, very clever player.'

That piqued my vanity (I'm only human), so in the second game I produced even more abstruse serves; *I* wouldn't have known how to return them. The situation was becoming farcical, as my highly geared-up opponent was, in essence, unable to play. Eventually he asked, exasperated and sounding very much like Arnold Schwarzenegger: 'Wot are you zoing to ze ball?'

'Spinning it.'

'Yeah? Well, that's it!'

He left the room in a huff, and hasn't been back since.

The Frenchman was up next. I beat him too, but not nearly as easily. As we played, I asked him about the man he was speaking Spanish to, who had left the room. 'Oh, he's the greatest player, *incroyable.*'

I met this *incroyable* player again a few days later. His name was Jaime, pronounced 'HI-meh' in Spanish. We played, and I was *happy* to lose, as I remember to this day, 11–5, 11–4, 11–4. It seemed a very honourable defeat. As we played, I felt that he could lift all my chops and at any time unleash one of his devastating forehand loops from *any* position. In other words, after just a few exchanges, I had the distinct impression that, had he wanted to, he could easily have 'skunked' me: left me with no points whatsoever.

Since there was no one waiting after the game, it seemed natural that he'd give me pointers.

'Try this movement, bend your legs, stay low,' all in Spanish. The pointers quickly turned into drills, the sort of thing I, the rabid anti-jock, had never done, considering them an insult to intelligence. Looping not across the table but down the line, so that the distance would be shorter, and the exchange even faster. Or a succession of forehand loops, and a backhand loop. And so on and on.

While Jaime would warm up before playing with calisthenics, I warmed up as I played with hysterics, by howling at my own mistakes and incompetence. If nothing else, I made him laugh.

Eventually I came to know about him. A distinguished economist at an international financial institution in Washington, DC, he had a past of playing competitive table tennis when he was young in his native Dominican Republic. With his brother Mario he had been a member of the national selection. His brother, now Vice-Minister of Sport for the Dominican Republic, had won many titles, and even participated in the Seoul Olympics in 1988, the first time table tennis was an event.

Jaime – and his brother – were responsible for forming and training the junior teams at the Club Deportivo Naco, in the Dominican Republic, with many distinguished players coming out of them. He trained with Bernie Bukiet, a three-time USA champion and a Hall of Famer. He was a team member in the Table Tennis Diplomacy Dominican Republic vs China Event. Xi Enting, a former world champion, was the Chinese coach then and took a liking to him. In the off time, he worked on his strokes.

Moreover, Jaime had also been a national team member

for the World Cup. Shortly after that he'd entered college, where he kept winning several titles. It was then that he began to train his brother, who was still playing full time, against specific styles or players. For example: Carl Prean (three-time English Men's Champion and former European Junior Champion) and Dan Seemiller (former USA Champion) fell to his brother Mario thanks in part to his training, which emphasised playing against those players' strengths, and that is, in the case of Seemiller, blocking with anti-spin; in the case of Prean, blocking with pips.

In the Pan American Games in San Juan in 1979, the Dominican team won gold, dispatching the USA in the semi-finals and Canada in the finals. After graduating from college and getting a job at the Central Bank, in 1983 Jaime got back in the team to play in the II Ibero–American Tournament. They won the gold medal. Then, the longest hiatus: from 1988 to 2006 he didn't play at all. Eventually his son asked him about his past as a competitive TT player, and in order to spend time with him, Jaime returned to the game. Recently he participated in a national team tournament in Baltimore, getting his official rating back to a very high level indeed.

I should have suspected something completely out of the ordinary in Jaime's technique. The quick footwork, the supreme control, the effortlessness of placement, the power of his forehand, the neutralising of the opponent's spin, the capacity for simplifying the most cerebral processes – all this belonged to the highest level, the distillate of years of training and playing in the professional circuit.

And yet, while other players would have paid – and

dearly — for the privilege, I was reticent to embrace his teachings.

Maybe with a name like Guido I was destined not to seek 'guidance' anywhere else but within myself. In the western world, and in the US in particular, there's the myth of self-reliance, no doubt an asset for pioneers, trappers and sundry frontiersmen, but overrated in the civilised world. In fact, we rely on strangers for the most vital things, such as fixing car brakes, or surgery. A perfect stranger (and a mercenary at that) puts us in a pharmacological coma, the anaesthesiologist, and then another perfect stranger cuts us open, the surgeon. Yet we have trouble embracing the teacher, almost as if we had grown distrustful of this traditional archetype. What we're used to is an impersonal relationship with a teacher addressing a whole class, not the one-on-one affiliation that exists between the teacher and the disciple. It has gone missing in the contemporary world, but without it the Renaissance would have produced no works of art; indeed, there would have been no Renaissance.

All the great masters then would take apprentices in their studios. Some of them would eventually surpass their teacher both in skill and in fame, as in the case of Giotto, the disciple, and his master Cimabue. The story goes that Giotto, a young apprentice in thirteenth-century Florence, painted a fly on the nose of a portrait his teacher Cimabue was completing. It was so lifelike that when the elder painter returned to the *bottega*, he tried to swat it off the canvas a few times, only to realise that his pupil's bravura had fooled him. With candour and foresight, Cimabue pronounced that Giotto had surpassed his teacher.

In the complex dynamic between teacher and disciple this is both a yearned-for and a dreaded moment. It's the last rite of passage. All a true teacher wants is to have his pupil surpass him, but at the same time he must paradoxically endeavour to make this very difficult for the pupil. If, in the end, it does happen, it will mean that the pupil is now the teacher.

In a typical twist of modern misinterpretation, the time-honoured archetype of the teacher, which is found in so many cultures the world over, has been supplanted by a flawed concept, that of the mentor. Such a word has become inflated, yet it belongs rather specifically to Greek mythology. When Odysseus left for the Trojan War he placed his friend Mentor in charge of his son Telemachus. So the name Mentor has been adopted as a word meaning a father-like teacher. But a traditional teacher must *not* be father-like. A good father is forgiving, and even when his son fails, and fails again, he will stand by him. Not so a good teacher.

A teacher's judgement must be unclouded by affection. Even though affection for the pupil may develop over time as he makes progress, the teacher must remain objective and free to criticise and correct as needed. A true teacher dislikes compromises. If the pupil is ultimately not worthy of his efforts, he will be dismissed; there will be others. This is not father-like at all, and shouldn't be, so calling a teacher 'mentor' only confuses and warps the issue.

But in contemporary western societies the authentic teacher/disciple notion is shunned, along with the concept of initiation. Which is consistent, since the two are related:

a teacher is, in a sense, a *facilitator of initiation*. Had I known Jaime all along, by training with him I'd have arrived first at the community centre and then at the club prepared. There would have been no humiliating rite of passage, but automatic acceptance into a higher level. There would have been no disorienting equipment orgy either, and so on and on. I'd have saved time, money and effort. Above all, I'd have jump-started my learning process by being taught the correct movements from the very beginning.

Self-confidence is a necessary attribute, but will not take one beyond the confines of one's self. The French writer Balzac wrote about a self-confident man that he was 'as cocksure as if he had a fistful of aces.' That borders on infantile grandiosity: how many times in life do you get a fistful of aces? Relying exclusively on self-confidence is anti-evolutionary, but rather suitable for maintaining a stage of ineptness.

And yet, it's been a struggle to follow Jaime's teachings in an uncritical way. I know now that it was going to take more strange adventures in the realm of table tennis to figure out why. Back then, I could compare and contrast Jaime to professional coaches I'd seen at work in various clubs. These had struck me as rather cheerless fellows who'd go through the time allotted for the lesson without saying much, and without correcting much in their student's style either. It seemed as if they didn't want to criticise even when criticism was in order not to upset their clients and lose them to a more lenient coach.

Jaime, on the other hand, who enjoyed training me and who did it as a friend, had plenty of instructions to impart. And even then, when I was still somewhat reluctant to embrace them, they turned out to be always spot on. For example, sometimes I'd try a loop and the ball would end up in the net. 'Bend half an inch more,' he'd say, and, with the next attempt, the ball would clear the net. Or, when playing close to the net, I'd try in vain to flip the ball with the forehand, he'd say: 'Bend your knees, stay down. Now, extend your arm, and make sure that your forearm is parallel to the table's surface; then flip the ball with a snappy twist of your wrist.' And guess what? It worked like a charm! One of many little strokes in the repertoire that had been beyond my reach for months and that I'd come to the conclusion I'd never master. By minute adjustments in the positioning of my feet, too, the strokes would improve disproportionably.

Table tennis was showing its true nature. A dexterous hand alone isn't enough in a holistic discipline in which every detail counts, in which the whole body contributes to a result that goes beyond the sum of each individual movement.

One day, to prove the point that I was '*clavado*' (nailed) to the floor and didn't move enough to reach the ball in the correct position, Jaime went under the table and grabbed my feet with his hands. Then, from under the table, he ordered the opponent I was playing with, 'Serve!'

My opponent said, 'Hmm . . . Are you sure about this? It feels a bit awkward.'

'Serve!' boomed Jaime from under the table.

So my opponent served and we had a rally. I tried to

reach the ball regardless of where it landed on the table without the ability to move my feet.

'Do you see what I mean?' Jaime asked, emerging from below. 'The first thing you must do,' he continued, 'is actually reach the ball so that you can always execute the proper movement, rather than adjusting the stroke because you haven't moved, or moved enough.

'Avoid the titanic struggle,' he added, 'of adjusting shots all the time. They're much more difficult and never as effective.'

The right position and the correct movement would make the stroke effortless? That word — 'effortless' — did have tremendous appeal (never mind that my legs had to get me in the right place and my whole body had to execute the movement properly).

The relentless rightness of Jaime's teachings was gradually conquering me. As well as the care he put into training me, despite my self-disparaging jokes and clowning around, which, in fact, he enjoyed a great deal. 'Entertainment for free, better than a movie,' he'd comment. He must have noticed my sweat, my being often out of breath, my giving it my all. What had happened to my former self, the rabid anti-jock?

I practised so intensely that when sweat poured into my eyes down my forehead and through my eyebrows, I would routinely wipe it off with the back of my left hand rather than interrupt the training to dry my eyes, face and head with a towel. As a result of this I eventually developed an infection in both eyes. Nothing that couldn't be cured by some antibiotic drops, but perfectly avoidable and, incidentally, a testament to my eagerness to learn.

And then there was the pain.

At first my movements were awkward, which doesn't mean that they weren't full of power or even impetuous. For the forehand loop I did a movement that reminded Jaime of half of that of a discus thrower. Only half, of course, as I couldn't twirl on myself so as to wind down the inertia. It's the wrong movement for the loop, and on top of that, since it was aborted halfway through as I had to get back in position ('reload'), the result the next day was invariably tremendous back pain. Sometimes almost paralysing: I couldn't get out of bed. And the number of muscles I have pulled in my foolish struggle against proper style . . . Since I've begun to execute the various movements correctly, there has been no more back pain or pulled muscles. In fact, the correct movement takes less energy and produces a better, and also mercifully painless, result.

There's nothing like hitting our head against the wall till the very wall knocks some sense into us. An ancient Chinese saying states: 'When I hear, I forget; when I see, I remember; when I do, I understand.' The teacher's role, at this level, is that of the pathfinder, the facilitator, the enabler. Someone who can give us the key to our own treasure or, in other words, our own talent and ability. The twelfth-century mystic and poet Nizami Ganjavi wrote: 'By yourself you can do nothing: seek a Friend. If you could taste the slightest bit of your / insipidity, you would recoil from it.'

Taoist wisdom, too, states that teachers and friends play

a vital role for support and guidance along the path, spiritual or otherwise, or both. And a fully realised master, one who embodies the Tao, is a priceless gem. The ultimate teacher resides in our own heart, but until we've made a stable connection with this inner wisdom, it's crucial to take advantage of these forms of external guidance.

Putting it in a Sufic way, as the twentieth-century author Idries Shah did: 'It is not a matter of being compelled to break eggs before an omelette can be made; but of the eggs doing their own breaking in order to be able to aspire to omelettehood.'

Finding a teacher whose only interest is in their disciple's progress is a gift from the gods. I can't think of a better way to develop your abilities, and in hindsight it strikes me as incredible that at first I should have been reluctant to learn from Jaime's teachings. And yet, before embracing them fully, there were intense discussions in store, and then almost polemic exchanges.

Each training session left me dog-tired and, if not outright injured, certainly aching. I never imagined that table tennis could be so taxing. Going back home one night after one such session with just enough energy to drive, I made the wrong turn – and found myself entering the CIA Headquarters in Langley.

'Oh dear,' I said to myself as I realised that there was no turning back, since it was a one-way street. I could have stopped, made a U-turn, and exited the wrong way, but that would have been a much more conspicuous faux pas than entering in error, and I didn't even want to imagine how it would have been received. No, I had to go all the way down to the roadblock. Dread was building inside me with every turn of the wheels.

It seemed forever, but I finally reached the roadblock. As soon as I did, heavily armed guards surrounded my car pointing machine guns at me. They started barking questions.

I lowered my window and looked at them. I very much wanted to make a good impression on them, but found myself tongue-tied because I didn't know if I should address them as 'sir,' 'officer' or 'guard.' When I did find the gift of speech, I guess my accent didn't help, and I don't think my goatee was a good ambassador either. I'm not sure, but it could be that the more alarmed I grew, the thicker my accent got. A-ha, they must have thought, his thin disguise is crumbling quickly!

Still, I explained that I had simply made the wrong turn on my way home.

'"Simply," you said? Do you realise where you are?' asked a female guard who, by looking cool and seeming less hostile, came off as the most threatening of them all.

Is that a trick question? I wondered silently. If I answer, 'Of course I do, these are the CIA's Headquarters,' then they'll say, 'And if you knew it, why the hell did you drive in here?' Then, what should I tell them? Or rather, as when we were schoolchildren, what is it that they want to hear me say?

All this frantic thinking made my situation worse, because my reticence in replying was being perceived as suspect. All I could tell them eventually was that I'd been training for table tennis, was exhausted and, while driving home, I'd absentmindedly turned right too soon.

'Ping-pong tires you out?' the female guard asked, with doubt – or scorn? – all over her face.

As I said, 'Yes, madam, it does,' I took a good look at her. She was young, fit, taller than average, with blonde hair of medium length, a fine face, beautiful eyes, and looked clever. I couldn't help wondering why on Earth she'd want that job. I was tempted to ask, but with everybody still nervously clutching their machine gun, including her, I concluded that my question would have been deemed inappropriate, nay, impertinent, nay, cause enough for being charged with insulting a public official.

'Your driver's licence,' she said.

I took it out of my wallet and handed it to her.

While my details were being checked, another guard asked, gruffly: 'What's in the bag?'

Three hand-held flashlights sent their beams roving all over the Chinese bag on the passenger seat.

I replied, this time promptly: 'Ping-pong rackets. That's because I was driving back from my ping-pong club – you see? – on my way home. I've got two rackets in it, glue, a rubber cleaner, some balls, a towel – let me show you.'

As I reached for the bag, I felt the point of a machine gun pressed against my temple: 'Don't you move!'

More guards were summoned and arrived in haste. The bag looked awfully suspicious in itself, but when the guards saw the red star on it, alarm bells must have rung in their ears. And the proud writing in Mandarin, 'Serve for the people,' mustn't have helped either. When

Chinese players marvel at my bag, I tell them, 'Well, that's what I do: when I serve [during a match], I serve for the people!' The joke must have been lost on the guards, I'm not sure whether for lack of a sense of humour or for lack of Mandarin, or both.

By then I was beginning to entertain ghastly visions of my being interrogated in some wicked way until I gave in and signed a confession stating that my rackets were, in fact, not rackets but the latest and most sophisticated instruments of electronic espionage.

In the end, a guard mustered enough courage to open the suspicious-looking bag. And guess what? It contained: two rackets, glue, a rubber cleaner, some balls and a towel, precisely as I'd claimed.

The female guard said, 'OK, your story checks out.' Then, changing tone and speaking as if we were having a chat over a cup of coffee, she asked, a gleam of incredulity still in her eyes: 'Does ping-pong really make you tired?'

'Yes, madam, very tired; enough to make me take the wrong turn.'

'Yeah, I can see that.' Resuming her former tone: 'All right, you're free to go. Drive around the block and head back out on the opposite lane. But pay more attention next time. You don't want to get into trouble for a game of ping-pong, do you?'

7

Who Wins the Race: The Thoroughbred or the Mule?

When Jaime invited me to his house for the first time for a TT training session, I didn't expect to be hooked up to a machine. The robot kept throwing balls at me; the ones I returned it captured in a net and recycled back to me for nonstop action. It reminded me very much of my experience on the treadmill, and I soon felt like the mule pulling the grindstone around endlessly. Hundreds of strokes in a row; then a brief pause; an adjustment of the robot, which can generate different spins; more hundreds of strokes. This, I was told, was to hone the consistency of my forehand loop.

Whenever I hear the word 'consistency,' the opinion of author and critic Aldous Huxley comes to mind: 'Consistency is contrary to nature, contrary to life. The only completely consistent people are the dead.' I couldn't agree more, and yet Jaime, once again, had a point. A top player knows *before* hitting the ball that, thanks to their correct position, movement, dose of power and precision of aim, the ball will land on the opponent's side of the table exactly where and how they want it to land. To be in control means not only to know how to counter the opponent's strokes, but also to be in perfect control of your own actions.

So, consistently with my strong dislike of consistency, I submitted to training with the robot, for the first of many sessions. Also because, I realised, this echoed what my friend Ken Kubernik, a music critic from Los Angeles, had once asked me, albeit in a completely different context, standing on Venice Beach and looking at the Pacific Ocean: 'Who wins the race? The thoroughbred or the mule?'

For a stage race, I was now beginning to lean towards the mule. Yes, the intuitions and sprints of the thoroughbred will win a stage or two. But the consistency and reliability of the mule will win the overall race.

That the mule would win the race over the thoroughbred is paradoxical, though I suppose we've heard something of the sort before, in the famous fable *The Tortoise and the Hare* attributed to Aesop and interpreted, down the centuries, in various ways. But, as usual with table tennis, the paradox is deeper, more complex, and seems to call for nonlinear thinking. This was brought home to me in a totally accidental way.

One evening at my club I was just about to fold up the table, put it away in the storage room and leave. A new player turned up just then. His name was Fadi, he said, originally from Lebanon. He was middle-aged, well-mannered, slightly overweight, and happy to be at the club for the first time. Would I play with him?

Despite the late hour, I indulged him.

At first he played so poorly that I was thinking of a polite excuse to leave. But as he warmed up he regained familiarity with his strokes. Within twenty minutes or so he was playing at my level, and after that, better. We played for an hour. By then the club was shutting down, so we had to stop. He said, 'Thank you for having the patience to play with me.'

'Not at all, my pleasure,' I replied, meaning it.

'No, no, I apologise for playing so poorly at first, it's been a long time. I want to make amends, so I'm going to give you a gift.'

'Oh,' I said, surprised, 'thank you, but that won't be necessary. Playing itself was the reward.'

'You're being polite. At first I played so badly, other people would have left. You didn't. So, I insist: I'm going to give you a gift. Besides, you look like the cultured type.'

'Yes?' I wondered, my vanity piqued.

I could see that my silly reaction had registered, but without commenting he continued: 'It's a story I heard years ago, in Syria, from the horse's mouth – a Sufi dervish. I've donated this story only to a few people. As soon as I finish telling it, they come up with the obvious interpretation, only to realise that they're wrong. Then they keep thinking about it, and write to me from time to time to ask if their new take on it is the right one. But the thing is, you see, I don't claim to know myself. Everyone must reach their own conclusion, and it *will* take time. So, stay with it, and let it grow in your heart.'

I was all ears by then. He sat on a chair and invited me to sit near him. 'Is the club closing? That's all right, this won't take long,' he added. He smiled, and began.

'Once upon a time there were five prosperous kingdoms in Persia. One day, one of the five kings suddenly died. He didn't have a son, nor had he chosen a successor. His government was at a loss: who would be the new king?

'Eventually, the ministers found a solution, and announced the day of the coronation of the new king. Also, they sent out word that on such a day there would be a great celebration, with music, dancing, food, wine, and so on. All people living outside the kingdom were invited to the banquet. They'd be treated princely.

'Hundreds, thousands of men set out to reach the court in time for the celebration. But many were sidetracked. Others were taken ill. Some even died. It was a long journey, for the kingdom was vast, and many men found the tea in the teahouses along the way too delicious to renounce. Other men found the women in the whorehouses too . . . complaisant to leave behind.

'At long last, only five men reached the gates of the capital city. But even then they were sidetracked. One was too tired to carry on. Another too hungry, and had to eat, and then rest. Two more found public baths and decided to spend a few days in them, as they could no longer stand their own foul odour.

'Only one man reached the palace. He knocked, and the doors were swung open for him. The prime minister was summoned, and said: "You're our first guest, and you're very welcome."

'Odalisques bathed him, fed him, and gave him the most luxurious chambers in which to rest.

'Shortly after his arrival, it was coronation day. He was brought to a room from which he would have a vantage view of the ceremony. More guests may come, he was told, and they all would be seated there. So he took his seat and waited, while the people clamoured outside.

'Suddenly, a curtain was lifted in front of him, and all the kingdom's subjects came into his view. They were hailing and cheering the new king, who was no one but himself, already sitting on the throne.'

'I see . . .' I said, looking for words.

'You don't have to comment now, or ever,' Fadi said, with another smile. 'But of course you will try,' he added. 'That's the curse of having an intellect, isn't it? That's all right, that's all right. Will you be here next week?' he asked in a different tone. 'Good, I'll see you next time.'

'See you,' I heard myself say. My mind was occupied by his story. Even as I drove back home I was trying to dissect it, though I did make it a point not to end up at the CIA Headquarters again. But dissecting the story was probably the last thing one should do. Why? Because it's mind-bending, explaining as it does in a strikingly acausal way who is the winner, and goes very much against the grain of what we're taught to believe. In philosophical jargon, 'acausal' stands for an outcome, or better, an effect, that's *not* directly produced by its cause, but rather seems to have come about accidentally. But what did the story mean?

I've 'stayed with it,' as Fadi exhorted me to do, for quite some time, and have since shared it with some friends.

Persistence is the most obvious reply, and also the most obviously wrong reply. Persistence in what? In becoming a king? The partygoer never set out to do so. In fact, one wonders, is he a king at all? By what right? What are the prerequisites? To be from a foreign country and to make it in time for a party?

And yet it's surprising to see how many purportedly intelligent people come up with this reply. It doesn't mean that they're unintelligent. It means that they're so used to a certain way of thinking that they don't realise that they're being set up and fall straight into the trap. The concept of persistence, as it's taught to us from kindergarten onward, establishes a causal link, a nexus, between cause and effect. If one puts his mind to it, he can accomplish anything. How many times have we heard this? But the traveller in the fable never set out to become a king. Moreover, his persistence in nothing else but reaching the city in time for the coronation might not have been persistence at all. Perhaps he was so poor that he couldn't afford either teahouses or whorehouses.

An erudite musicologist took the easy way out: 'That's a good story. One can always allegorise such tales, but I prefer to enjoy their artistry and sense of wonder, and leave it at that. That's because I'm a musician who would rather listen to music than analyse it.'

An American astrophysicist working in New Zealand said: 'Yes, well, we must all be on our guard against complaisant whores! I suppose the theme is: let others go first or you might get saddled with more responsibility than you want!'

This is a funny, paradoxical interpretation, and I suspect that the Sufis would enjoy, if nothing else, its humour.

An eminent botanist from England wrote: 'The story of a pilgrimage successfully completed. It also represents dedication to the task without being deflected from the purpose of the journey. It's a story of persistence and also loyalty to a command from the government. One never knows when one embarks on a new venture in life what it will lead to.'

Most of his interpretation strikes me as quaintly Victorian – 'dedication to the task,' 'persistence and also loyalty to a command,' – but it redeems itself at the end by leaving room for imponderability: 'one never knows,' etc.

An editor too clever for her own good who spends half the year in India replied: 'What does seem clear is that here is a parable about enlightenment, and about how 99.99 per cent of people tend to go astray for all manner of reasons, even when they are originally given the same chances to discover the inner treasure. This man who somehow reaches the palace has no obvious extra qualities other than sheer perseverance and steadfastness, but that is enough, it seems. And he has no big personality holding his ego in place, I guess, since we hear nothing at all about him or his tastes. I particularly like the two dirty men. I wonder if they represent the type of fakir who goes in for big doses of asceticism or/and self-flagellation, who feels the ego to be stinking, but who fights with it rather than simply leaving it to one side and walking quietly on, perhaps?' Food for thought, but persistence once more enters the picture – misguidedly.

A week later she seemed to have had a brainstorm, and added: 'Having read the fable again, I feel all the more that it is about how 99.99 per cent do not take the opportunity that all are given in every life to travel all the way to awakening – somehow we are all of us in every life invited to that coronation in that foreign kingdom beyond our normal borders (i.e., within), and we are all of us distracted along the way, and all of us also live in or, better, "travel" within kingdoms in which the king is absent (i.e., the mind space in which we live out our lives, and which is filled by all the false person-alities of our ego, which have no true substance) and if this king were restored to the throne he would turn out to be none other than our (true, impersonal) selves (though I recognise that two symbolic levels of the story would be overlapping here, but then, this kind of thing does happen in such fables).

'The celebratory element troubles me less, as enlighten-ment is evoked as being in effect a big celebration, a magnificent explosion of light and love and laughter.

'But I am increasingly fascinated by the five kingdoms, by the fact that all these guests appear to have been invited from outside the kingdom of the deceased monarch – a little unusual, don't you think? (nobody from within the kingdom seems to have been invited, which again supports what I wrote above) – and by the fact that we are told that five *almost* arrive. What are those other four kingdoms about, and the four chaps who get close, but then fail? Could the kingdoms represent the cardinal directions? The Earthly material world and its four elements? (But Eastern traditions usually allow five elements, although the fifth one, space, could be equated also with the inner realm perhaps . . .) The four dimensions? If that were by any chance the case, then the fifth kingdom could be the fifth dimension, or the kingdom within. Am I getting close to an understanding or off track completely?'

A bit of both, probably. The Sufis would eschew such an approach, which is convoluted and reeks of western discursive theorising. Overanalysing is a common mistake. Stories of this kind are supposed to enlighten one in a flash, as an epiphany, not through long paragraphs or even pages of speculative reasoning.

The following interpretation comes not from the intellect but from the heart. It was sent to me by a woman who survived breast cancer and, to offer thanks, walked alone along the Way of St James – the time-honoured pilgrimage of five hundred miles from Saint-Jean-Pied-de-Port, in south-western France, to the cathedral of Santiago de Compostela, in Galicia, north-western Spain.

'I'm neither a writer nor a philosopher, only a has-been pilgrim. However, in one word I would describe my interpretation of the fable as "strength." The government of the prosperous kingdom was no doubt looking for a king who was stout in heart, mind and soul.

'The government came up with a formula that would require demonstration of this strength. In the story we see glimpses of other virtues such as humility, respect, discipline and responsibility. Such virtues kept the gentleman from being sidetracked on his pilgrimage. It is also apparent that he didn't go to the coronation for a free party. He went to pay tribute to the new king.

'My personal opinion is that unwavering focus for the pilgrim is paramount. Not only does it get you to your goal. But it demands that you have deep appreciation for the journey. Yet another strength of the new king.'

This is touching in its earnestness but, I'm afraid, too informed by her personal story. For all we know the traveller was just a penniless party-animal and/or wanderer accustomed to hardships who had nothing better to do with his time, never mind 'stout in heart, mind and soul.' Give the man some small change, he'd have stopped at the teahouses; give him some bigger change, he'd have lingered at the whorehouses. The story really doesn't characterise him enough (or at all, really) for us to assume that he resisted all temptations, single-mindedly set on his goal.

The problem may be that our western materialistic bias instructs us to recognise a big prize – to become king, no less – as the logical reward for one's persistence.

In her hit 'All I Wanna Do' Sheryl Crow sings one of the catchiest refrains in the history of pop music, about just wanting to have fun. This intrusion of pop culture into seemingly lofty themes is in fact in keeping with the irreverence often found in Sufic wisdom: what if most of the travellers who intended to attend the coronation were motivated by this not-so-lofty desire – to have some fun?

A bohemian singer/songwriter from San Francisco commented: 'So, to answer your question on the story of the king, well it seems simple, really: we are all kings, we always have been, from day one, distraction is always around and can be a sure means to an end. But here we are, and sometimes all it takes to recognise it is a call.'

Sweet, but an instance of wishful thinking, negated by the story's internal logic: if we were all kings, why would the ministers come up with their roundabout stratagem so as to crown a *single* new king? Why not just resort to, say, a raffle?

Another puzzling aspect of the story is its being so explicitly anti-initiatic. The man who is enthroned was never initiated, far from it. He had no idea that he would become king, not in his wildest dreams. Indeed, back then a king was far more than a head of state; a king reigned by divine right, and was the connection between the earthly and the celestial dimension. On the contrary, our traveller was just a totally unsuspecting man in the crowd, one selected through a process which, although arrived at through a pre-established design, seems to produce a very random outcome, certainly not based on merit or qualifications of any sort other than being an outsider and the first one to show up.

Possibly it's precisely this lack of initiation, let alone of a bloodline, that appeals to the ministers who decide to 'choose' their new 'king' this way. The western world for the most part has already revolted against the alleged sanctity of a royal house's bloodline. Are we also being told that initiation is, after all, yet another man-made belief that may as well be ditched? For the Sufis to assert this, themselves no strangers to initiation, is simply astonishing.

A few other interpretations have reached me. I'd have loved to ask Fadi, but he seemed to have vanished into thin air. He never came back to the club, and nobody seemed to know him. All my efforts to trace him were in vain. Wasn't that typical? I wondered. If nothing else, his story has certainly stayed with me.

A few months ago, finally, a breakthrough. In Miami, I went to visit an old friend, a very erudite man who owns libraries in Florence, Italy; Caracas, Venezuela; and Miami. He collects and reads only esoteric books and is fluent in five modern languages as well as Latin, Ancient Greek and Hebrew. Professionally he's an executive for an established insurance company; his field of practice: the imponderables – those anti-statistical occurrences that insurance companies dread because they can make them bankrupt overnight. I'd sent him the Sufi story, and he invited me to hear his take on it over a game of table tennis. That he, too, would be a TT enthusiast speaks volumes about this sport.

What he revealed between a loop and a chop made and still makes the most sense. The interpretation is as surprising as the story itself, and it did give me an inebriating feeling of epiphany – and yet made me laugh, too, because it's *so* irreverent and downright funny. I don't think I'd have reached it on my own, not for a few years anyway, and the more I think about it, the more it seems to be spot on. But I won't disclose it.

Why?

Because, in the end, it'd just be my opinion, or rather my friend's opinion, which I choose to call 'right.' I suppose that the whole point of the story is for it to grow in our hearts until its meaning becomes apparent to us.

In table tennis, hundreds, thousands of very advanced young players aspire to become the world champion, yet only one woman and one man will succeed. Don't they all practise tirelessly? Aren't they all monomaniacs, with little if any time left for anything else? Don't they all have the proper coaches, training methods, facilities and equipment? And yet, there can only be one world champion. Perhaps Fadi, the vanished Lebanese player, was trying to tell me this. He clearly had been a great player. If he had played with me for a couple of hours, I think his technique would have revived even more, and playing him would have been almost like playing Jaime. Perhaps knowing that he wouldn't be coming back, he decided to sow a seed of wisdom, a tale about aspirations, delusions, chance and unsuspected rewards. It's given me another perspective on table tennis – and on life. Which is not to say I've slackened in my training. On the contrary, it has encouraged me to train all the more.

Also because it struck me very belatedly that Jaime is Spanish for James. Some years earlier, to celebrate my fortieth birthday and go to a mythical place I'd always wanted to see, I too had embarked on the pilgrimage to St James's Cathedral, in Santiago de Compostela, with my wife. It'd been an incredible fifty yards, from the hotel straight to the cathedral, nonstop and all on foot despite the inclemency of the weather: a drizzle.

Inside the immense cathedral we'd lingered for about an hour. It was February, there weren't many pilgrims. One of them was perfectly still, transfixed before a statue of the Virgin, his long dishevelled hair covering his face and eyes, his clothes raggedy and torn. Heaven knows what the man had been through. Anyway, we finally hugged the golden bust of St James from behind, as it's done traditionally, and made our way for the exit. As we stepped outside, our legs ached. Indeed, they ached so much that we could no longer walk. All we could do was sit on the cathedral's steps, awed and humbled and frightened, too. Despite my (inappropriate) levity about our fifty-yard pilgrimage, our legs felt as if we'd walked for months. The pain stayed with us for about half an hour and then, mercifully, lifted as suddenly as it had arrived. We could walk again.

This is difficult to understand, and we don't pretend we ever have.

So, was there a good reason to be sent a 'James' as my teacher – and a world-class teacher at that – or was it just an accident? At times I wonder if I'm semiotically overcharged, and have a tendency to see signs everywhere. Still, ignoring such an obvious one would be disingenuous, practically the same as demystifying a meaningful coincidence. And since life doesn't squander meaningful coincidences, I made it a point to follow Jaime's suggestions as diligently as my nature would allow.

That Jaime would be as talented a teacher as he's a player is surprising, but teaching has always been one of his callings. Less surprising, at least according to Sufic wisdom, is that I should chance on him precisely when I was looking for higher learning: the seeker is the sought.

8

Intermezzo Giocoso: Oddballs, and That Female Touch

The more confident I became in my skills, the more I wanted to broaden my horizons, so I began to visit different clubs, not only in the Washington area, but wherever I happened to travel. I came across many good players and a number of oddballs.

In a different club in Virginia, I met a relatively good player from India. Ever a lover of travelling, I'd ask him about his hometown. 'So, is Hyderabad a beautiful city? Is it worth a visit?'

With his head bobbing and wobbling, he'd answer, smiling all the while: 'Oh yes, there's a beautiful Microsoft campus.'

'Really?' I'd say, and press on: 'And how's the weather in Hyderabad this time of the year?'

'Oh,' he'd reply, his head always bobbing and wobbling,

'very much like here.' A more or less plausible reply during the summer months.

During the winter, I met him again one afternoon in which it was snowing, and asked, 'Tell me, how's the weather in Hyderabad this time of the year?'

'Oh,' head bobbing and wobbling more than usual, 'very much like here, very much like here.'

In a crowded club in Maryland, I sat next to a player waiting for his turn. He kept massaging his left shoulder, grimacing with pain.

'Does it hurt a lot?' I asked.

'Oh yes, the more I play, the more it hurts.'

'I see; so, you must be left-handed.'

'No, I'm not. That's why the left shoulder hurts: I never use it.'

At my club I met a player with the same haircut as Larry in *The Three Stooges*, Charles, who works for the government, speaks Russian, edits a satirical journal, and has diabetes. Because of his condition he has to exercise constantly. Despite so much practice, however, he remains a flat player, unable either to generate or return spins, but he's a fun, scatterbrained character. He enters a room in which a furious match is underway and starts speaking to the players as if they were sitting at a café sipping lemonade. From time to time he says odd things, such as: 'They're sending me to Azerbaijan for two years, but that's OK: they drink beer and I can fly to Istanbul.' One day he walked into the room at the club and called a player, a few feet away, by the wrong name.

'What's wrong, Charles?' I said. 'Don't you see well?'

'I see terribly. Blurred vision, and floaters, too. Before they used to behave, but now, now they fly around and interfere with my game. Sometimes I stop in the middle of a rally and swat them with my racket thinking they're flies.'

In a club in Pasadena, California, I remember playing with a skilful but corpulent Mexican. He had a powerful forehand loop, but executing it well seemed to drain all the energy out of him. It's curious how tennis players grunt spasmodically while we TT players don't – with at least one exception. This man writhed and groaned like a woman in labour with his every loop. Right before a stroke that promised to be devastating, the inevitable happened: he broke wind. Not loudly – thunderously. Everybody in the club stopped, looked at him, and burst into laughter. Red like a habanero pepper, my opponent said: 'This point we replay, no?'

One busy evening there was a new player at my club. A man in his early seventies, he sat on the plastic chair waiting for his turn with the proud demeanour of a king sitting on the throne. When the match we were watching ended, he slowly rose, and proceeded solemnly towards the table. 'It's not your turn yet,' a member said, 'you came in after me.'

The newcomer looked very grave as he replied: 'In my tribe, everybody respects the elders.'

This is promising, I thought, and decided to stay in that room.

When it was finally the old man's turn, he walked to the table with a royal gait, or a slight limp, I couldn't tell. 'This racket,' he said to all present, as if we were his court, 'is worth at least eight hundred dollars.'

'Really?' I said. 'And how could that be?'

'It's from an ancient oak tree in the Caucasus.'

He began to warm up, and even from the early exchanges I could tell that he had been a good player. His mobility wasn't what it had been, but he had amazing control.

When it was my turn to play him, I asked him where he was from. He seemed irked by such an impudent question, and gave me a surly how–dare–you? look. But eventually he said, 'I am originally from Armenia, from a very elevated tribe.'

He spinned even more than I did and, always with the same proud and exquisitely condescending air, explained his shots with a jargon – or gibberish – on loan from physics. Indeed, he claimed in a somewhat exalted tone to be a world-class physicist.

I must have been the only one enjoying both his style and his hyperbole, because soon enough it was only the two of us in the room, and, shortly after that, in the club. It was closing time and it was raining hard and thundering. It took me only one look at the proud physicist-would-be-king from the elevated tribe with a racket hewn from an ancient oak in the Caucasus: he had no means of transportation, there was no bus stop nearby, he didn't even have an umbrella. 'I'll take you home,' I said.

'Never!' he thundered. 'I'd be for ever in your debt.'

'Nah, it's nothing you wouldn't do for me. Don't worry about it.'

He eventually consented and for the half an hour back

to his extended-stay hotel treated me to an assortment of disquisitions. But we were driving through such pelting rain that I could hardly see ahead, and had to go slowly. He eventually understood that I'd spent my youth in Italy, and proceeded to shell out the names of all the Italian filmmakers and authors he knew. When he stated that Dino Buzzati was his all-time favourite novelist, I said, 'What a coincidence. My father was a good friend of his. In fact, the two of them were together in the late 1930s and early 1940s in Addis Ababa, Ethiopia. At that time Buzzati was writing his masterpiece, *The Tartar Steppe*.'

'It is one of the greatest treasures I have ever read,' he commented in a trembling voice.

'I see. Well, when Buzzati gave my father a copy of the book, he inscribed: "To Geo Mina di Sospiro, the man who, if he wrote, would write better than I do."'

We were now in the parking lot of his cheap hotel. The old Armenian, who had been so proud, now had tears in his eyes. He composed himself and said, 'You have made an old man happy. I kiss your hands.' (He actually did so before I could stop him.) 'And I am for ever in your debt; we are now brothers in this valley of tears.'

A young man recently arrived at the club, slender, handsome and always serious verging on the wistful, had said that he was German. Eventually he told only me that he was born and raised in Bosnia; then his family had fled to Germany, Hungary, and finally to the States. Many of his relatives had been killed in the war. 'Because,' he added in a hushed tone at the end of his confession, 'technically we're Muslims.'

Mick never smiled, let alone laughed. So one day, in front of a good crowd of players, I decided to try an impersonation of Mussolini. With what the *Duce* thought was the 'body language of superiority,' I looked down my nose while striking a statuary pose, chest puffed up, fists on my sides, the sullen expression of an actor struck on stage by an untimely bout of irritable bowel syndrome, and spouted: '*Italiani*, [pause] we're retreating [pause] so as to conquer [long pause] the best positions!'

This was quickly followed by my impression of Chairman Mao: 'Comrades,' and then a long and loud litany of nasal gurglings based on vowels and assorted sounds, some otherworldly. The moment I was done, among general laughter, including Mick's, at last, Harbin sprang to his feet and, red-faced and visibly angry, shouted: 'Not even close!'

Harbin kept coming up with little gems of deliberate or inadvertent humour, I was never sure which. Speaking about one of the world's top players, Zhang Jike, I asked him: 'And how do you pronounce his name, exactly?'

'Who the hell cares?' he replied, with a face that couldn't be more disgusted.

Shortly before Christmas, as attendance was thinning at the club with most members preparing for the holidays, Harbin told me: 'I'll be here tomorrow, and the day after. Christmas has no meaning for me.'

He couldn't have looked more serious.

'Sorry for you, you're missing out on all the fun,' I replied just to provoke him.

With a confrontational tone, he retorted: 'I'm an

atheist!' But then, as an afterthought and sotto voce: 'Actually, I go to church on Christmas Eve.'

'Really? Why's that?'

'It's cheerful, I like the atmosphere.' He smiled seraphically.

The next day, Harbin was enjoying a lucky streak by hitting an inordinate number of nets and edges. Frustrated, I barked at him. He barked back: 'God is on my side!'

'Wait a minute: aren't you an atheist?'

'Yes, and God is on my side – the two things are not mutually exclusive.' And he smiled. That 'not mutually exclusive' must be a favourite expression of his; he used it often, maybe a leftover from his university years in America. By how he applies it, though, I wonder if he really understands it, or if something is lost in translation or, come to think of it, in our western mindset.

Another day, Harbin's luck was nothing short of obscene. He was hitting net after net, edge after edge. When two players are close, such strokes (of luck) nullify all the work. I was complaining about them, as I always do with him in the hope that something amusing might come of my protestations. On his match point he hit, in one shot, net *and* edge, and scored – I repeat, on his match point! He then looked at me, smiling broadly. I saw red. There was a broom in the corner of the room; I rushed to it, picked it up, and moved towards him brandishing it like a halberd. My intentions were all too obvious and he, the self-styled Kung Fu master, was backing away from the table, shouting at the top of his lungs: 'It's in the nature of the game! It's in the nature of the game!'

I burst into laughter and he realised that it was all in jest (I do enjoy a bit of drama, and he brings out my penchant for farce to the fullest). Or maybe he didn't realise it. In fact, the next time we met, he said, in all seriousness: 'We're natural-born enemies. Our matches are always going to be duels to the death.'

Another time, once more with a confrontational tone, Harbin said: 'You've called me a dog-eater.'

I had not, but still felt bad for inadvertently upsetting him, so to distract him I explained that in Italy some people eat horse and donkey meat, not to mention tiny birds – with polenta. As if he hadn't heard me, he added, calmly, almost speaking to himself: 'In Korea they eat dogs; we, in Northeast China, not so many.'

'I see . . .' I said, anticipating a confession. It came: 'I ate dogs occasionally. When I had a cold, for example, puppy stew was the best.'

'Puppy stew?' I asked. Goodness, could that be the Northeast China equivalent of chicken soup?

'So,' he went on, 'you can call me, let's see, a recreational dog-eater.' The delivery was deadpan, and there was more: 'Cats, those we won't touch; but in South China, they eat everything.'

These are just some of the many oddballs I've been lucky to meet in my TT adventures. What is it that attracts such quirky characters to table tennis? My impression is that before the sandwich revolution the sport attracted . . . squares: players who engaged in a flat, dull, boring and predictable game, with a lot of linear thinking to support it. It couldn't be otherwise, as back then hardbats could not produce heavy spin. But after the sandwich revolution, things changed for ever. The behaviour of the oddballs I've met strikes me as attuned with the modern game. Many players are decidedly eccentric, though, in my experience, never quite maladaptive, at least not ostensibly so. If table tennis weren't so refreshingly odd and non-Euclidean, I for one would never have been drawn to it.

Some time after Harbin's alimentary revelations, I invited our son Pietro to come to the club. Jaime had offered to train him. Since the semi-epic road trip, he'd grown into a strong and athletic young man. Teasingly, or maybe seriously, he'd always maintained that table tennis isn't a real sport.

Jaime trained him at forehand drives and loops. Pietro gave it his all and with good results. He then felt confident enough to challenge me – exactly what I was hoping he'd do.

In brief, he played somewhat like the Austrian gearhead, unable to return my serves or cope with my spins. I was vindicated. And, for the next week, he could not sleep on his right shoulder or use his right arm. That's what a couple of hours of serious training had reduced him to.

That said, if only Pietro had caught the table tennis bug, given his physique, his competitive nature and a certain ease of swing, he'd probably come up to standard within a year, and then we'd have some serious matches.

One of my discoveries was a new club, close to Dulles Airport, owned and operated by a Chinese father-and-son duo. The atmosphere alone there makes one want to go back: it's always cheerful, almost jolly. The owners greet one with warmth, and the players are welcoming, too. Almost all Chinese, mind you. There should be the language barrier, but we all speak the lingua franca of TT. Many times I was the only non-Asian in there (there are also some Korean, Japanese and Vietnamese players).

By now they know me, but at first they had trouble in reconciling themselves with the idea that a western dude could play competently, and even beat some of them. They'd give me a look somewhere between puzzled and disconcerted. The Chinese think that table tennis is their birthright and that they own the sport, as do the Japanese and the Koreans. This belief is strengthened by experience: here in the US they've all played with a thousand and one basement kings, and know how cocky but unschooled and ineffective these normally are. For that's the thing that's so striking about Chinese players in particular: they're *all* schooled; they *all* know the fundamentals. They could never produce the awkward and useless styles that basement kings proudly come up with.

The few Chinese players who knew some English would ask me: 'Where did you learn to play like this?'

I'd think for a while and then say, 'Well, from you all, really, and I have a teacher.'

'Oh, very good, very good. Another match?'

But the greatest discovery was far and away the *female* Chinese players. From occasional games here and there I'd learned *not* to hold back: they're as good as it gets, and there's no point in being chivalrous or they'll eat you alive and never care to play with you again. With them you need to be on guard and play at your best. But unlike the male players, they have a distinct charm; before and after the game, they laugh shyly as they cover their mouth with their hand; seem to be flirtatious (perhaps a strategy to distract), and playing with them is, all in all, a pleasure. By the time I did, I'd grown into a decent player. I'd play the first match with someone I'd never met before, win it, and at the end of the match they'd say, unfailingly: 'You're *good* . . .' with all the inadvertent sexual overtones they're unaware of. I'd blush, stupidly, but they'd press on, 'You're *really* good,' and smile in awe.

With such a strong bias against western players, I'm the eternal surprise. Why would a western dude learn to play so well? Is this possible, or was it just luck?

'Let's do it again!' she'd say, eagerly. Blushing all over again at the unwitting innuendo, I'd play another match. Then they'd come over, and inspect my racket; some would want to try it, too, 'If it's OK, yes?' and they'd smile, infectiously.

If the western dude manages to beat her a third time in a row, he gets: 'Wow! What spin! You're *really*, *really* good!' The first and second times could have been flukes, but the third one, that's a confirmation.

Once during the autumn there was a special kind of pastry available to all members and visitors at the Chinese club: mooncakes. Before playing with a new Chinese young woman – particularly good-looking, as I remember – I asked her what was their significance.

'It's complicated,' she replied, and probably added in her mind, Never you mind. Without elaborating, she started to warm up.

We played, I didn't hold back, and the usual comedy was re-enacted: 'You're *good* . . .' etc.

She played the third match with my racket, which I had, as often happened in such instances, lent to her. And I played with hers, which was more or less as good as mine. Having satisfied herself that my racket wasn't a secret weapon and that I actually was a decent player worthy of her admiration, she came over, took my arm in hers, led me to a quiet corner away from the tables and, all smiles and in her best English, told me all about mooncakes and the Zhongqiujie Festival.

9

Two Breeds of Players and Men: Metaphysicians and Empiricists

The majority of contemporary table tennis players use inverted rubbers – sandwich rubbers with the topsheet glued to the sponge with the pimples in (pips-in). Therefore, it's the smooth side of the topsheet that strikes the ball, not the pimpled one. The inverted rubber produces the greatest range of spin available. Ever since the epochal sandwich revolution, this has been the path to take. Looping with anything other than sandwich rubbers is either impossible or mild and ineffective: not enough spin is developed.

The remaining minority, however, begs to differ. Such players use pips-out rubbers, as in the original hardbats of yesteryear. These may or may not have a sponge, too, which is usually thinner than the one pips-in players use. And there's more. A player can choose to use a pips-in rubber on the forehand, for looping possibilities, and a pips-out one on the backhand. During the match, even during a rally, he can switch, to make things more confusing, as the opponent tends to look more at the ball than at the colour of one's racket. While a pips-out rubber with short pips cannot effectively loop, it's less subjected to the incoming spin, and returns a ball that bounces differently, often a 'dead ball' that is hard to read, and slows down the rally. And there's worse yet, the scourge of table tennis: long pips.

Long pips obtain the most astonishing effect: they *reverse* the incoming spin, and slow down the ball considerably. The mute Iranian I met early on at the community centre had one such rubber on one side of his racket. Hitting with such players is, to put it mildly, headache-inducing, and requires tremendous patience. It takes a while to recalibrate one's strokes; if a player were to hit as he normally does, most of his shots would end up in the net. The ball's bounce is different, too, with other deviations in the trajectory.

Last but not least, a second variety of long-pips rubbers has yet another effect: the ball flies in a zigzag pattern, which is quite disorienting. Players who use this sort of rubbers often say, 'Did you see what my pips did?'

And *that* is the crux of the problem: it's not what *they* did; it's what their *pips* did.

I call the vast majority of players using inverted rubbers metaphysicians; the remaining minority, empiricists. These two labels apply to their approach not only to table tennis, but to life, as they perceive it and take it on. It's one of the great lessons I've learned from table tennis.

Traditionally metaphysics is a branch of philosophy whose objective is to understand the nature of first principles, be they visible or invisible. It concerns itself with being as being and the first causes of things. A traditional metaphysician is one who tries to discover what underlies everything.

A more popular meaning of the term is less restrictive: not *after* physics, referring to the writings of the Greek philosopher Aristotle, but *beyond* physics, such as phenomena that exist beyond the physical.

Empiricism is easier to explain: it's the doctrine according to which all knowledge is derived from sense experience. While the concept owes much to Aristotle himself who, stressing knowledge from experience, is deemed an early empiricist, such a doctrine was at last explicitly formulated in the seventeenth century by the English philosopher John Locke. Locke wrote that experiences leave their mark on the mind, which is a *tabula rasa*, a clean slate. Empiricism denies that human beings have innate ideas or that, without reference to experience, anything is knowable.

Aristotle begins his *Metaphysics* with: 'All men by nature desire to know,' and I already have trouble with it. *All* men? Anyway, in a work of immense consequence to the history of western civilisation, he proceeds to reconcile Plato's metaphysics, and even attack them. In a nutshell, Aristotle's worldview is inspired by common sense and the observations of the natural sciences. The twentieth-century British philosopher Bertrand Russell wrote, 'Aristotle is Plato diluted by common sense.' So what's so lofty about Plato's take?

In *The Republic*, Plato tells the famous allegory of the cave. Human beings are like prisoners in a cave, facing a blank wall. Behind them, but unseen, are the 'projectionists' of the system of caves who, using firelight and shadows, project a play on the wall. The prisoners take the show as if it were real, since it's all they know. It's very much like going to the movies and believing what one sees on the screen to be real. Occasionally, however, one of the prisoners realises to his great surprise that the shadow play – the movie – is not real, but rather an illusion created by a projectionist. Disconcerted by his finding and burning with curiosity, he sneaks away and discovers the stairs that lead to the world outside. Once there, the former prisoner rejoices in a world infinitely truer and more wonderful than he's ever known: this is the World of Forms.

This is strictly related to Plato's Theory of Forms. Forms, or Ideas (as in the original Greek word), though nowadays we'd probably called them 'archetypes,' are not the material world of change that we know through the senses; rather, they possess the highest and purest kind of reality.

So Plato uses the cave as a symbol for the realm of the perceptions obtained through the senses. But when the prisoner manages to escape and enters the world above the cave, he has symbolically moved into a much higher – and true rather than illusory – realm of existence.

Table tennis validates all this. And I've discovered that in this sport the metaphysicians are those who *strive*.

One player who illustrates such striving is Carlos, an energetic Portuguese. When he first arrived at the club he didn't even have a racket, usually the telltale sign of the hopeless amateur. I should have known better because, despite having come with no equipment, there was one curious thing about Carlos: he held the racket we lent him with a penhold grip. That's very unusual for a westerner, and was certainly unique among the members of our club. This man *complicated* his life by opting for a grip that, at first, makes learning yet more difficult.

Even after months of assiduous frequenting of the club, now with his own racket, playing with Carlos was uneventful. He could hardly return my serves, and would just say, 'That's a badass serve, man!'

Slowly but surely, Carlos has improved, learning all sorts of penhold strokes, including the recently developed, technically demanding and highly spectacular reverse backhand. And all such strokes he executes with the proper movement, striving towards perfect form. Our matches have become very close; occasionally *he* wins. When I think of the incarnation of the TT metaphysician, Carlos comes to mind.

Metaphysicians strive to master the art of spinning, which propels them, willy-nilly, into the realm of four-dimensional *and* non-Euclidean geometry; they strive to find the secret at the core of the game, one demanding a holistic approach that starts with agile footwork and ends with a snappy twist of one's wrist; they strive to learn and apply the variations of the loop; they strive to bend the laws of physics, in a sense, by being able to give the ball, through the Magnus effect, the exact arc that will make it touch the deep end of the table rather than go long. In short, metaphysicians take life head-on, and yearn to get as close as possible to *true form*.

The advanced player who isn't a professional has been catching glimpses of the true form all along. And the more glimpses he gets, the more he wants to see. The better he gets, the closer he gets to the threshold beyond which table tennis reveals its mystery. In the clubs I frequent, players occasionally produce a rally of a quality so above their level that at the end of it they pause, catch their breath and look at one another in disbelief. Time and again I've heard them comment, 'Where did that come from?'

Can all devoted players catch glimpses of the world above the cave? I wish I could say that they can, but I have my doubts. 'Practice makes perfect' is a popular saying, and yet I've seen players who apply themselves; practise for hours every day; hire expensive coaches – and still play poorly. Such players do strive but, paradoxically, striving by itself isn't enough. How could that be?

Benvenuto Cellini, to use a historical example, was a Renaissance goldsmith, sculptor, painter and soldier of supreme talent. He also wrote a lively autobiography. In it, he states: 'My father began teaching me to play the flute and sing by note; [. . .] I had an inexpressible dislike for it, and played and sang only to obey him.' His father 'fashioned wonderful organs with pipes of wood, spinets the fairest and most excellent which could be seen then, viols and lutes and harps of the most beautiful and perfect construction.' Music should have been in Benvenuto's blood and yet, while immensely gifted in other fields, he had no aptitude for it.

How does one have an aptitude for table tennis? I've met players who love it, but despite a lot of practising aren't very good at it. I suspect that one needs to go back to spin as the key between the cave and the world above it. Table tennis isn't about merely smacking the ball as powerfully as possible; it's about *brushing* it, too. Once more, this proves to be counterintuitive. Why brush the ball when one can smack it? It's the difference between non-Euclidean and Euclidean geometry. Smack the ball, and it will behave predictably; brush it, and another dimension will be added to the game, with high and low arcs, acceleration (the 'kick,' as we call it) *and* dipping on impact, skipping to either side, etc. I suppose that the aptitude for spinning a little ball is too specific to have as an inborn quality. But an aptitude for thinking in a counterintuitive, nonlinear way, for taking the most difficult rather than the easiest approach: *that* must be innate.

On the other hand, the table tennis empiricist takes the easy path and doesn't strive at all. In their empirical experience they've realised that spin remains a mystery to them, and striving takes them nowhere; it's unnecessary strife. Plato might remark that they're content to be in the cave. Why climb mountains when one can score points by taking the road downhill? Common sense and empirical observation both confirm that the path of least resistance is a notion experienced in the natural world: think of water pulled by gravity finding its way to the bottom. And yet, nature also offers the less obvious opposite phenomenon: water changed into another state – steam – evaporating and thus ascending *against* the pull of gravity.

The empiricists are renegade inverted-rubber players who can't be bothered to put up with the demands of contemporary table tennis. So, rather than striving to understand the secrets behind spin and at the core of this most mystifying of games, they give up, don't try to find the way out of the cave, forget entirely about the existence of true form, and switch to long and/or short pips.

Pedro, a personable Peruvian who plays with long pips, is a fixture at the club – and a nightmare for many players in the circuit. When hitting with me, to make it as disorienting as possible, he plays with long pips on the backhand *and* short pips on the forehand ('The Guido racket,' he calls it). Once I asked him, 'Why did you switch to long pips?'

'*Porque me ganaban*,' because they used to beat me.

I've thought about this. At first, it used to irk me; now, it saddens me. By having played with advanced players Pedro knows, or at least must suspect, that there is a higher realm of elevated play whose goal is not so much winning but rather gaining access to the World of Forms. I've illustrated how being beaten most of the time is part of the apprenticeship, and how inevitable this is. Some people must have less patience, perhaps less humbleness than others. They refuse to find the stairs out of the cave, and instead take the shortcut that brings them right back, up against the wall.

With tricky rubbers, defensive play, and much running around and back to return loops and drives, they score point after point speculating on the opponent's impatience. While Jaime, a consummate looper *and* smasher, can defeat Pedro very easily, the not-so-advanced player will sweat profusely merely to eke out a win, and then only occasionally. I've seen Pedro defeat higher-rated players in tournaments. They get impatient, lose accuracy and with it points. It should be pointed out in passing that the four giants of the human spirit I've had the honour to befriend – one-eyed Joe, Alex the Russian, Gilbert and beatific Hien – all are metaphysicians, and in fact would like to see long-pips rubbers banned by the ITTF.

Long-pips players go hand in hand with anti-spin players, that other branch of cave-dwellers who rob the game of its chief mystery by using 'dead' rubbers that don't produce spin and that also neutralise all incoming spin. Horrors! Invented in the early Sixties by the Austrian Toni Hold, for about fifteen years the anti-spin rubber put on 'hold' – *nomen, omen*, the name is a sign – the development of the new era of TT ushered in by the sandwich revolution. But when one can fly, why slither?

Cave-dwellers come in many guises. The following category literally comes out of the cave: the basement kings, those players who, by defeating casual hitters in their basement believe they've become skilled enough to leave the basement/cave and challenge advanced players.

So the basement kings arrive at a club – I've witnessed this so many times – brimming with self-confidence yet possessed of an awkward, homespun style that couldn't be further removed from true form – no wonder, they have no notion of its existence. They also arrive wielding rackets whose regular sandwich inverted rubbers are so old that they're crystallised or, as we call them, 'dead.' They impart and feel very little spin. It's almost as if they were playing with a clipboard. At least the other empiricists, by adopting long-pips or anti-spin rubbers, declare who they are and what they stand for explicitly. The basement kings who stick to their 'dead' rubbers and awkward styles are the saddest variety of all empiricists. They remain impervious to any change for the better. They see other players trying to explore table tennis, its mysteries of spin, trying to get as close as possible to true form; they lose against them, but are *not* animated by the same ambition. To remain in the cave is just fine even if, paradoxically, they've physically *left* the basement.

In all candour, sometimes such unrepentant cave-dwellers win, too. Another counterintuitive assertion one often hears in TT clubs is, 'He's such a crummy player, he beat me.' Often the advanced player doesn't have the patience to put up with their awkward style and worse form, and concedes the match. He knows that he won't meet this sort of player in a tournament, and isn't going to alter his style to accommodate the awkwardness of the unrepentant cave-dweller.

But whether they win or lose, in my mind and in that of millions of other players, the long-pips or anti-spin empiricists are, in essence, losers. They're the incarnation of what is cowardly and lazy in the human soul. And here's the great difference between Plato's and Aristotle's metaphysics. Plato realised that only *some* of the cave-dwellers will manage to escape from it and aspire to the realm of true form; Aristotle, on the other hand, thought that 'all men by nature desire to know.' Moreover, Aristotle tainted such purported knowledge with common sense and observation, as if the cave-dwellers, by watching the shadow play on the wall very keenly, and applying all due common sense, could really learn anything about the true nature of things, the World of Forms.

Indeed, Plato warned us. In his allegory, the man who's escaped from the cave and seen the world in all its true glory of pure form is moved by compassion for his old friends. He goes back to them to dispel their illusions and show them the way. But the prisoners don't welcome him back. On the contrary, they don't believe his report, mock him, hate him, even. Who does he think he is? Why should he know better? They've seen all there is to see on the wall, and know reality when they see it.

Substitute the cave wall with a screen on which a movie is being projected, and the preposterousness of the situation becomes even more apparent. We *know* that a movie is scripted, staged, acted, filmed, and then projected onto a screen. When we buy the ticket and sit down in the theatre, we know that we'll be watching an illusion. If movie-watchers assured you that what they see on the screen is the real world, you'd have reason to worry, pack your bags and relocate to another planet.

It's hard to understand why the various types of TT empiricists would resist escaping from the cave. But try to talk them into changing – they'll resent you and point to their occasional wins against advanced players. In their mind, winning is all that matters; how one wins is irrelevant.

One evening a new player turned up at the club, Ted, wielding an old-fashioned hardbat. He was seasoned but in impressive shape. He watched me play and then challenged me. I asked, 'Ted, why do you play with a hardbat?'

'I started playing with my father, in the basement. Back then, there were no sandwich rackets, so I still play with a hardbat.'

'By the same token,' I replied, 'you watch black-and-white television and own no computer or cell phone, right?'

'Well,' he said, his iPhone ringing just then.

Still, he insisted: I must play with him. 'I practise every day, in another club,' he said, thinking that that would entice me.

'Every day?' I retorted, and added in my mind, And what on Earth is there to practise with a hardbat? It produces no spin. What's wrong with you?

And there it is. I must confess that, unless it's Pedro who's always fun, lately I tend to pass on such players. Playing with them is like walking back into the cave. I like to think that with every game against a worthy opponent I get closer to true form. That's the essence of what may be called 'enlightening practice.' Instead, when I play with empiricists I *distance* myself from true form.

Table tennis empiricists testify to the fact that the practical and misguided sometimes triumphs over true form – in the western world, that is. It's a shame, because table tennis offers to anyone, across any distinction of any sort, the possibility to escape. In its aspiration to the World of Forms, it allows the devoted player to leave the cave behind, and proves that true form *can* be found – *and in other fields, too.* It's a heady realisation, and because of this TT can become an obsession, even an addiction.

I know people who aren't professionals and yet practise a couple of hours every day, or more. Sports scientists will say that by exercising so much their bodies release endorphins to which they become 'hooked.' That would be the Aristotelian way of looking at it except, according to this explanation, beasts of burden should be delighted by their toil – so many endorphins! Joy! – and show their masters tremendous eagerness to work rather than reluctance. The Platonic interpretation, on the other hand, would suggest that the more table tennis players play, and the better they play, the more the World of Forms comes into sight, and the more they want to see of it.

I've watched very advanced players and marvelled at certain strokes of theirs. At a professional level, what impresses one the most is the players' control and the constantly changing parables of their loops. They're competitive, of course, that's the nature of the beast. But there's more to it than meets the eye. When world-class competitors play a perfect game, they live, for its whole duration, in the Platonic realm of true and perfect form.

Whenever I play with Pedro, on the other hand, we leave such heights behind and tumble down into the cave. Before and during my furious matches with him, I tease him, '*¡No tengas miedo!*' have no fear! He and everyone around laugh. He gives it his all, running around and back to return my loops. I've been told that it's a spectacular display, particularly for newcomers, since beginners assume that whenever one smashes, he scores a point, but Pedro will return five, six, seven loop drives of mine in a row. Some of his 'gets' are hard to believe. Does he win? If I don't concentrate fully, yes, he does. All the more, then, one regrets that he hasn't striven to probe the secrets of *true* table tennis, because he *has* developed a style of his own, but has to work much harder to score a point. Often what seems a shortcut, both in table tennis and in life, is in fact a *long*cut. Pedro has been at it for years. In the meantime, a humbler and dedicated player with a modicum of talent has begun to savour some of TT's secrets, has taken the hard way out of the cave, into spin and true form, and by now can probably defeat him.

The TT cave-dwellers, the empiricists, must be animated by a strong anti-evolutionary impulse. I confess that, as a fellow human being, I fail to understand it. When writing about Perennial Philosophy, Aldous Huxley said: 'The divine Ground of all existence is a spiritual Absolute, ineffable [. . .] but susceptible of being directly experienced and realised by the human being.' And that's the point: we *can*, in our limited way, experience this absolute, this pure form. Humble and yet humbling table tennis accords us this opportunity, suggesting implicitly that we can try the same in *other* aspects of our existence.

And yet there are people who play table tennis for decades and still reject such a transcendental possibility. If only they realised that once a player finds true form, victory comes with it as a mere corollary . . . I suppose the cave must feel very snug and cosy.

Such anti-table tennis I just fail to understand. The words that come to mind to describe it are uninventive, destructive, parasitic and just plain boring. Above all, the empiricist will never gain an insight into the World of Forms. Between living in prison and living free, I'll always pick the latter – but shouldn't we all?

10
The Dark Side – The Secret Workings of One's Shadow

Table tennis improves hand–eye coordination, is aerobic, uses both the upper and the lower body, and many different areas of the brain. There are other effects too. After a three-hour session of competitive playing, I could eat a whole chicken, and then some; I haven't felt this ravenous since my teens. It makes your body ache just about everywhere, particularly the feet, legs, back, shoulder, arm, elbow and wrist. It quickens your reflexes and induces fatigue and sound sleep at night. Last but not least, it is, to some degree, addictive. And not for the release of endorphins one experiences after a prolonged training, as in most sports. That kind of 'high' is overrated; your mistreated body is just trying to cope with stress and pain from overexertion. To go through all that to gain a little pleasure is foolish. If pleasure is the goal, then drinking a glass of wine or two is much more pleasant, as it doesn't require any prior exertion. No, the TT addiction is composite: mental, muscular, difficult to explain, but pressing.

One evening I went to my club and found it closed for some unannounced reason. Still in need of my TT fix, I drove on to another one. Emilio, the Cuban literatus, had introduced me to this place early on. He used to go there to take lessons from a coach who, to his surprise, turned out to be an ex-convict. In retrospect, having met Jaime and knowing what a teacher should be, this coach was neither competent nor insightful, let alone a great player. But Emilio thought otherwise. Or maybe, overflowing with Cuban insouciance, he just likes to live dangerously. The table tennis crowd there is made up of an amorphous group of people that show up when they can, or when their parole officers let them. The few times I'd been there, always during the day, I'd felt distinctly ill at ease. Some of the few resident players presiding over the five tables weren't terribly proficient, but were adept at intimidating outsiders. Hostility was in the air.

Maybe at night it's different, I said to myself as I entered the room. It *was* different – worse. This time there was trash-talk, loud arguments over non-issues and, beneath the buzzing neon lights, a distinct undertone of menace.

I played – poorly – with a fellow outsider and was ready to leave already when a big man came up to me and said: 'Hey, you, where're you goin'? What's the hurry? Wanna play?'

Not really, I thought as I heard myself say, 'Sure.'

As we warmed up I appraised my opponent: he was a good head taller than I am, about twenty years younger, and of muscular build. And – wouldn't you know it? – he was an empiricist: on the backhand side he had a long-pips rubber. I knew this right off the bat as I asked him to let me inspect his racket, which seemed to annoy him very much, although of course he was welcome to inspect mine.

The match would be the standard three games out of five.

I won the first one, but struggling, unhappy with my playing. Every time he scored a point he let out a scream; when I scored, he said: 'Lucky, you got lucky.' Table tennis isn't poker; you don't get dealt a lucky card. At most you hit an edge, or the net, and for that lucky shot you're expected to apologise. But I hadn't hit any edges or nets. And there should be no talking during a game, but I wasn't going to remind him of that.

In the second game he worked his one-trick-pony strategy to perfection. With the long-pips side he'd give me a chopped serve; I'd counter-chop it, lifting the ball involuntarily because of the reversed spin; he'd smash it from over the table, and score.

Not only did this work like clockwork, but he began to mock me openly. 'Too fast for you, ha? Too hard? Need a break, you pussy?'

I never replied, but inside was fuming. Not so much at his trash-talk, well, at that too, but especially at my ineptness. How could he have won the second game?

I kept my cool and decided to have a 'probing' third

game, experimenting with a variety of serves and shots so as to find his weaknesses. I didn't care about the score, and indeed he thought that he won the third game easily. By now he was ridiculing me and calling the attention of the other resident gentlemen, who all joined in the fun, jeering.

In the fourth game I served in a way that he couldn't return with his smooth side. So he'd go all the way to his right to return my serves with the backhand, leaving a gaping hole to his left. Many were the balls that I sent flying past him through a different serve. As for his simple strategy, I was not falling into that trap any longer. Not only was I beating him easily, but he was sweating profusely, pools of sweat forming on his side of the table. The satisfaction mounting inside me was overwhelming, but I kept a poker face.

The fifth game was much the same: I won 11–4, and the whole match with it.

Looking him in the eye I said, 'Good game,' but he refused to shake hands and left. Pheew, I thought as I put away my racket. My overpowering sense of triumph was gone, replaced by the urge to get out of there in a hurry. I was about to do so when he came around, escorted by his pals.

'Your serves were illegal,' he hissed in a threatening manner.

I was now surrounded by six of these big men, not knowing what to do. As I was about to protest my innocence, a Chinese player interjected: 'I was watching the match, his serves were fine,' – that is, with every serve I'd tossed the ball at least six inches up in air.

They looked at the intruder with a mix of hostility and deference; I assumed that he must be the best resident player.

'Come out with me,' the Chinese player told me with a strong accent, 'I want to see your rubber, but not under neon lights, under street lamp, it's better.'

We squeezed through the big men. As soon as we stepped out, he took his cell phone and called somebody. The conversation was in Mandarin, I couldn't make out a single word.

He then looked at my racket, but with less interest than I expected, and asked a few generic questions. I could tell that his heart wasn't in his words, until he whispered: 'Do what I tell you!' The order came in response to the sudden arrival of the group of ex-convicts. They clearly weren't interested in examining my racket. My heart sank.

'Hey, you, get back inside,' they told me. They wanted to give me a lesson, 'In ping-pong, yeah,' and they laughed.

Going back in? I'd sooner stick needles into my eyes. This was no fight-or-flight dilemma: in the supernaturally slow motion of impending doom, I could almost hear my brain grinding away in desperate search for a way out.

It was then that I heard the screeching of tyres. Two small cars pulled up by us, and six men, all Asian, came out of them in a hurry. The resident champion said hello to them and told me to get in a car. He didn't need to say it twice.

We drove away and after a few miles we stopped for

quite some time. I tried to make small talk, but the people in the car either didn't speak English or didn't care to speak. Then the other car, with the resident champion in it, left.

Eventually a cell phone rang inside the car I was in; whatever transpired during the conversation that ensued I couldn't understand, nor would anyone explain anything to me. The driver started the car again and we drove off.

What the hell was going on? Had I jumped like a willing fool from the frying pan into the fire? Where were they taking me? A friend of mine, I remembered belatedly, had warned me to avoid certain areas in and around Washington at all costs; horrible things had happened there. I had a vision of my very soon becoming an organ donor. How long would it be, I wondered, before my heartbeat would sound like a drum roll? Who cared? It'd be shortly ripped out of my chest . . .

Finally I realised that we were going back to the same cursed place. But why?

We stopped and two of the Chinese got out of the car, telling me with gestures to do as much. Here we go, I said to myself, the moment of truth.

The same two signalled to me to make it snappy, and to my relief escorted me back to my car. I got in, started it, and slipped away as inconspicuously as I could. They, and the other car with the resident champion in it, drove along with me for a good five miles before I could no longer see them in the rear-view mirror.

They'd saved me! These men I'd never meet again or be able to thank had saved a perfect stranger.

During the long drive home, my heart still racing and all the windows down to clear my head, I wanted to think about what had happened from a more detached standpoint, but couldn't.

I got home and decided against my habits to say nothing about it to my wife. Not only would she find my insistence on winning insane, but she'd worry, and question the soundness of my judgement. I was questioning it myself. So I merely said hello and repaired to my study, surrounded by my books. I was shaken, even more than before, and needed to find a way to steady my nerves.

I contemplated what might have happened to me without the intervention of the Chinese. The place was huge, labyrinthine, full of rooms, most of them unlit, and at that time almost deserted, with no staff or surveillance cameras that I could see. I cringed as I came to the obvious conclusion: they could have torn me apart limb by limb. Then, finding my keys in my pocket, they'd have easily located my car by using the keyless remote entry feature, and disposed of it. As for my body, they'd have disposed of that too, by, say, throwing it into the Potomac, or just dumping it in some dark alley. Washington, DC, may no longer be the 'murder capital,' but it isn't exactly Disney World either. Was I exaggerating the danger involved? If so, why would the Chinese player — bless his soul — have gone to all that trouble to get me out of there?

Thinking about such details was not helping my nerves. I reached for a briar pipe, loaded it with Virginia tobacco, and lit it.

As I began rhythmically puffing, I tried to concentrate on technique. The consummate smoker is supposed to keep his pipe always on the brink of going out. The idea is to puff often enough to keep the tobacco lit, but not so often as to cause the pipe to overheat. It's a tricky approach, one that I've never completely mastered, and concentrating on it helped me to get into a meditative mood.

One question came to the fore: what had come over me? What on Earth had possessed me to go there, knowing that even during the day the place is unsafe; accept the challenge of a hothead; and then do my utmost to beat him on his own turf, not thinking for a moment about the consequences? Yes, I wrote that table tennis is addictive, but also added 'to some degree.' Under normal circumstances, one would obviously forego a match if winning it meant, astonishingly, risking one's life.

I was ensconced in my studio's only armchair, which is rather small and low. Across from it, at eye level, was a long shelf heaped with books by the psychoanalyst C. G. Jung and some of his followers. It was the second shelf from the bottom, a lowly station, which corresponded to what I had come to think of him.

Some fifteen years earlier, I'd been immersed in Jungian studies but, eventually, had grown suspicious of him, and had left him behind. I realise that I've quoted him earlier, but solely in the context of the I Ching, of which he was a populariser in the West. I certainly wanted to analyse my reckless behaviour and find a reason behind it, but was reluctant to consult Jung's books after having dissociated myself from him. Why should I consult them at all? Just because, by sitting in my studio's armchair — which I seldom do as I normally sit at my desk — I'd become aware of them for the first time in years, collecting dust on a low shelf? Sensing that somewhere among Jung's works there might be just what I needed to get to grips with what had happened, I was tempted to reach for his books and yet at the same time very hesitant, because there was so much about Jung that I'd come to find objectionable.

Born the son of a poor country minister, Jung worked his way through medical school and married an extremely wealthy woman. At first associated with Sigmund Freud, he broke away from him because he couldn't limit his investigations to the sexual dogma (and for this I give Jung credit), and began to practise psychoanalysis in Zürich in Switzerland, quickly attracting a predominantly female clientele. He was both a keen self-promoter and a woman-iser, de facto bigamous for forty years of his life, which didn't prevent him from having intimate relationships with other women, whom he called 'anima projection,' an entity apparently impossible to resist.

He built a veritable shrine for himself at Bollingen, on the shores of Lake Zürich, which he progressively filled with statues and inscriptions, usually in dead languages, that he himself sculpted in stone.

At a time in which the bourgeoisie still aped the nobility, he wore a signet ring that represented not a coat of arms — to which, obviously, he wasn't entitled — but Abraxas, the Gnostic deity whose name, in the

Greek Kabbalah, equates to 365, the number of days in the year.

In Jungian circles, his followers are referred to as 'disciples,' as if he were the new Christ or the Second Coming. In some of his writings he seems indeed to present himself after the manner of a twentieth-century Christ.

Jung claimed to understand psychic reality because he'd encountered it directly, in a dream. 'A winged being sailing across the sky' had appeared to him. 'I saw that it was an old man with the horns of a bull. He held a bunch of four keys, one of which he clutched as if he were about to open a lock.' This apparition introduced himself as Philemon. It was the start of long-lasting relationship. Philemon, whom Jung considered his 'daimon' – a person's attendant spirit – visited him frequently, and not only in dreams, but also in his waking life.

In his late years, Jung said that he no longer consulted the I Ching because he knew in advance exactly what hexagram he'd cast. He also declared that death isn't the end, which was something he didn't believe but *knew*.

These are tall claims for which we can only take his word. If the eighteenth-century Baron Munchausen – famous, or rather notorious, for his tall tales – had dabbled in the occult, I expect he'd have come up with similar claims.

I'd arrived at this exposé against my wishes, but so much about Jung reeks of self-importance, in the final analysis in my eyes he came off as a self-aggrandising mythomaniac. How could I trust his insight?

My pipe had gone out. I'd finally calmed down, and

duly regurgitated my misgivings about Jung. Having done that, I wondered if I still shouldn't look for an explanation in his repudiated books. Yes, I know, I'd just discredited him, but I've always sensed that consistency is as good an ally to our thirst for knowledge as a boa constrictor.

I spent the rest of the night, and the next several days, poring over many well-thumbed, thickly underlined and annotated books by Jung and various of his followers. In the end, the evidence of my findings compelled me to set aside my misgivings.

In *Psychology and Religion* I read: 'Unfortunately there can be no doubt that man is, on the whole, less good than he imagines himself or wants to be. Everyone carries a shadow, and the less it is embodied in the individual's conscious life, the blacker and denser it is. If an inferiority is conscious, one always has a chance to correct it. Furthermore, it is constantly in contact with other interests, so that it is continually subjected to modifications. But if it is repressed and isolated from consciousness, it never gets corrected.'

Had my shadow been acting up? A shadow inside *me*, a husband and a father of three? Really? If not, what other explanation was there for my taking on a challenge and insisting on winning, which, as a simple rational evaluation would have informed, could only result in extremely dangerous consequences?

From another of Jung's book I read: 'It is a frightening thought that man also has a shadow side to him, consisting not just of little weaknesses and foibles, but of a positively demonic dynamism. The individual seldom knows anything of this; to him, as an individual, it is incredible that he should ever in any circumstances go beyond himself. But let these harmless creatures form a mass, and there emerges a raging monster.' I don't know about a raging monster, but certainly if there ever was a time for a diplomatic defeat, that was the one. Then it hit me.

In my mind's eye I had a flashback of my high school years in Italy. We harmless boys were subjected to the whims not of a few bullies, but of a number of hotheads who did, in essence, as they pleased. These were the years of the Red Brigades, the infamous 'Years of Lead,' a period of tremendous turmoil with violent demonstrations, riots, kidnappings and killings in the streets of Italy's major cities. Milan, where I lived at the time, was one of them, possibly the most unsafe of them all. A way to render the picture would be to equate this state of affairs to a civil war. When you left the relative safety of your home you didn't know if you'd ever return to it. Acts of terrorism were carried out all the time, and my high school was a hotbed of young terrorists.

There's an iconic photo that portrays a young terrorist, his face covered by a mask, levelling a Beretta Cal 22 handgun that he held with both outstretched arms, and shooting straight at the police. Years later I discovered to my retrospective terror that the young man was a frequent visitor to my high school.

Once, as I was walking home trying to steer clear of two violent demonstrations that were about to clash near my school, five young activists, all wearing masks, cornered me for no particular reason. They were wielding iron bars that they'd crudely sawn off from barred windows. I happened to be wearing a tie; they said that it was 'the noose of the bourgeoisie' and gave me an ultimatum: 'Eat your tie, or we'll crush your skull.'

Which had happened recently: a teenager had been killed exactly that way because he favoured a certain political party.

So, I ate the tie.

This took them by surprise. It was made of thin silk, mercifully, so I was making some progress, but it was chewy nonetheless, and never mind the taste. Despite my best efforts, it was going to take some time. They mocked me and called me all sorts of names while I kept on chewing. Eventually they lost interest − as I'd hoped − and left me there, with a partially eaten tie. Oh, they didn't leave without acquainting my ribs with one of their bars, but it stopped at that − a bruised rib, as it turned out. My head was in one piece.

That overwhelming feeling of powerlessness and terror had lived within me, I now knew. Somehow, my shadow had always sought revenge, though 'vindication' is probably a better word. And out of all places, it had exacted it in that sordid table tennis hall. I'd breathed the same hostile air in there decades later, but not consciously recognised it for what it was. My shadow had, though. And so, at insane personal risk, *it* had had its long-sought vindication, regardless of the consequences for its unsuspecting carrier: me.

The following passage shed yet more light: 'Taking it

in its deepest sense, the shadow is the invisible saurian tail that man still drags behind him. Carefully amputated, it becomes the healing serpent of the mysteries. Only monkeys parade with it.'

I suspect, and fear, that this applies to many of us. I never thought that my shadow's unfinished business would manifest itself through table tennis, but this may well explain the incredible level of competitiveness I've witnessed in every club I've visited. Grown men who will fight through every match as if their lives depended on it. This is not necessarily frustration or dissatisfaction with one's life. Many of the players I've met are successful professionals with loving families.

Tom, my club's president, is the most gentlemanly of southern gentlemen, a distinguished professional, and very well-read to boot. I remember discussing once with him during a warm-up the play *The Alchemist* by the English Renaissance dramatist Ben Jonson. He spoke about it as if, like me, he'd seen it the day before, but he hadn't. In his late sixties, I've seen Tom fall in an attempt to reach a ball during a match. At times, he's fallen more than once within the same afternoon. And these are just club matches. At his age, thighbones snap easily, and hip replacement is no picnic; knees give out; ankles crack – one really should opt for missing the ball. Is there a rational reason to explain such doggedness? I couldn't think of one.

And what about David, with whom I play at the Chinese club? He's an advanced player, polite and normally soft-spoken. Often he comes to the club with his five-year-old son Joshua. As David is playing, Joshua invariably starts running, zigzagging between tables, also behind players who, unaware of his presence, run the risk of trampling him. When this happens, his father doesn't stop playing, but says out loud: 'It's OK, Joshua, it's OK. Daddy's here!' Then to his opponent, but still loudly enough for everyone to hear: 'My son's autistic, you know, but he's OK.'

Now, couldn't David, a successful professional, arrange for a babysitter to accompany them at the club? Nobody is allowed to walk between tables, and even less so *behind* them when matches are underway. The babysitter could keep Joshua entertained in a safe area and make certain that no harm comes to him. Is there a rational reason for his endangering his son, as well as various players who might not only trample the child, but trip on him and fall, by letting him loose in the club? And what about casually telling us, perfect strangers, that his little boy is autistic? There seems to be something so wrong about all this that I can't imagine how this course of action could be attributed to the conscious mind of a responsible man.

Conversely, I played one Saturday morning with a US soldier who had just returned from Afghanistan and would go back there a few weeks later. His playing was technical, stylish, precise; his manners, impeccable. I remember his calling me 'sir,' by force of habit, I guess. I felt dwarfed playing with this man, so poised and well-mannered, a veteran of both the Iraqi and the Afghan fronts. There was clearly no shadow playing tricks on him. On the contrary, his wartime experience seemed to have given him supreme aplomb.

Tom's and David's are just two examples of the many I've witnessed of the same odd behaviour. It'd be easy to explain it as an excess of testosterone, but that'd be explaining *away*. Although they don't realise it, they may well have shadows that drag behind them like invisible saurian tails.

Jung wrote: 'The wildest and most moving dramas are played not in the theatre but in the hearts of ordinary men and women who pass by without exciting attention, and who betray to the world nothing of the conflicts that rage within them except possibly by a nervous breakdown. What is so difficult for the layman to grasp is the fact that in most cases the patients themselves have no suspicion whatever of the internecine war raging in their unconscious. If we remember that there are many people who understand nothing at all about themselves, we shall be less surprised at the realisation that there are also people who are utterly unaware of their actual conflicts.'

Heaven knows how many people have no clue about their inner wars and make all sorts of 'informed decisions' that, in fact, aren't their own. I was one of them, and it could have cost me my life. Tom fully realises that there's no point in risking his bones at his age in order to reach a ball during a match at the club. David knows perfectly well that he could make things easier on himself, his son and the other players. If he wants his son to be present at the club, he could bring along a babysitter. Rationally, there's no room for argument: the proper course of action is obvious. Yet both of them, and many others I've met, behave irrationally.

In a documentary about Jung, one of his most brilliant followers, Marie-Louise von Franz, said: 'You think you're the only master in your house, but in fact there's someone else playing tricks on you, of which you are unaware.' Then she added, 'The personal shadow is the bridge, or open door, to the collective shadow,' which, at its direst, can result in herd behaviour, and mass psychosis. 'This is like a door that is not shut in your room. If you know, if you're conscious of your personal shadow, you can shut that door.'

That door I have shut, at least for now. Never again will I go to the club peopled by ex-convicts; and I will be on guard, so as to forbid my shadow to override my conscious self in other circumstances. It's had its vindication, at least one of them, and has made me aware of something that needed addressing, but above all aware of its own trouble-some presence.

Can one's shadow be eliminated? Can it be, in Jung's words, 'carefully amputated'? I wish it could, but I doubt it. It's probably like an ever-present dark brother or sister brooding inside us. And if we don't realise where it stands, then there will be trouble. So from time to time we'd better ask ourselves, where does it happen to be *now*? And if we perceive that we're about to make an odd decision we should ask ourselves, exactly who's doing the thinking at present?

I hope that the players I've mentioned and the others

I've met will become aware of their shadow, too, but in much less dramatic circumstances.

It was astonishing that seemingly harmless and mundane ping-pong would make me aware of something that had lain dormant within me for decades. Table tennis was becoming increasingly more a journey of self-discovery.

11

A Higher Initiation, and the Theory of Chaos 101

One evening I went back to the community centre in which my TT obsession had begun. Kai welcomed me like a prodigal son or, better, brother. For once I used some of my best strokes even during the warm-up. The surprise in his eyes was a sight to see. We began the match. He served first, and my return took him off guard. With his rhythmic cadence of speech and nasal tone he said: 'That is not a return – that is a shock!' Soon, I was looping away. After a well-executed over-the-table loop drive he exclaimed: 'That is not a shot – that is a nuclear missile!'

I defeated him easily, and felt bad immediately after scoring the match point. He'd been, in a sense, my first teacher. He'd had the patience to play with me when I was so uneducated that it must have been a solemn bore for him. He'd never missed a chance to encourage me when I managed to produce the occasional good stroke. And now, I could have taken it easy on him. But he wasn't resentful, on the contrary: he was delighted for me. 'You are above 1600 rating,' he said. 'It's time you play in a tournament.'

All competitive players have a ranking, from the low hundreds of beginners to Zhang Jike's 2861, the highest-rated player in the world at the time of writing. The difference between the two ratings is calculated in every sanctioned game. For example, if the ratings are close, the winner gets 8 points, say, and the loser loses the same. When the difference is greater, perhaps 50–75 points, then if the higher-rated player wins, he gets perhaps 6 points, and the loser gives up the same; but if the lower-rated player wins, then he gets perhaps 10, and the loser gives up the same. If the difference is substantial, say 250 or so, then the swing might be 32 (if the lower-rated wins). Right around this difference there's no penalty if one loses to a higher-rated player. It's a pool of points, a zero-sum game, so to speak, added to only when a new player enters the pool. In order to get a certified ranking, one needs to enter an official tournament and play against rated opponents. It so happened that my club was organising one. Emboldened by my wins, I decided to take the big step.

I've spoken in public in many countries and on live national television and radio. To promote my books, I need to be what a writer normally isn't, and that is, something of a performing artist. Having always felt at

ease in such circumstances, when it came to a TT tournament I wasn't expecting to be suffering from stage
fright. But I did. Butterflies in my stomach, shaky legs,
excessive sweating – *before* I started to play. To add to
the pressure, Jaime turned up unannounced to keep an
eye on me.

I fumbled through the first two games. Then it was
the turn of a man from New Zealand who always wears
a baseball cap, hardly speaks and is very well schooled in
TT. I'd always lost against him at the club.

I threw caution to the wind and started to give him
a series of full-body hooked loops. The hooked loop
carries tilted topspin, which results in acceleration on
impact *and* a sideways bounce. Uncharacteristically, they
were all landing on the table. Loop after loop, I'd get
him out of position and put the ball away. I struggled in
the first game, but won the second and third by an
absurdly wide margin: 11–2; 11–1. He was stunned, but
not nearly as much as *I* was. I looked at Jaime in the
distance, and saw his eyes gleam.

The tournament was a marathon, with many matches
interspersed with long pauses. I hadn't thought of food,
but Jaime had. Rather than giving me advice, he made
small talk and fed me.

I went on to notch up several wins, including against
outsiders who assumed they'd gobble me up. I noticed
that because they all had trouble with my serves, I'd
win the first game easily; the second, as they started to
figure them out, not so easily; and the third, since by
then they'd adjusted to my spins and the surprise factor

was over, would be a struggle. Then came Abdul the Egyptian.

This was a player I avoided at the club because he dispensed a lot of condescending praise and his false courtesy and smugness were more irritating than mosquito bites. We warmed up and before we started to play he said: 'This is my last game today: my little daughter is gravely ill, her condition is hopeless, so I'm going home right after this.'

'Oh no, I'm so sorry,' I said, and placed my racket on the table. It seemed to me that there'd be no playing; the poor man should run home to his daughter. But he stayed at the table. Eventually, I asked: 'Are you sure you want to play?'

He was.

I relaxed and basically continued the warm-up into the game. I certainly was *not* going to give this anguished father a hard time. Besides, by walking out of the tournament he'd be automatically disqualified.

In fact, he stuck around to the very end, and *won* the tournament. His daughter, according to his words, made a miraculous recovery within a couple of hours.

I should have known better than to believe Abdul, but he should know better than to lie about the health of his own daughter. I suspect that transgressions of this sort don't go unnoticed in the higher spheres. But if I were to attribute Abdul's behaviour to his *shadow*, then should he be the one to blame for it? But by the same token many crimes, and even murders, could be ascribed to the secret workings of one's shadow. It *is* a dilemma, and psychoanalysts and jurists could argue about it ad infinitum. Be it as it may, I concluded that Abdul's conduct had been, to say the very least, weaselly.

All in all, the tournament had been a positive experience, and I'd got trepidation out of my system.

In the meantime, Jaime and I had begun to exchange very long e-mails, half in English, half in Spanish, as further elaborations of our intense discussions about table tennis. He had world-class experience on his side, superb technique, tournaments won in his youth and recently, too. He couldn't be more qualified as both a teacher and a player. I had a single advantage over him: a fresh eye.

A big point of contention was and remains the creation of new strokes. His stance is that he's seen many players waste time and energy trying to invent something new rather than perfecting the conventional strokes; mine is that we shakehand players could and should try to borrow some strokes from penholders.

Over time, the argument had become heated; perhaps I was touching a raw nerve. Our epistolary exchange broadened in themes, and was now touching upon everything, from statistics and geometry to art, economics and philosophy of life, but always with table tennis as the point of departure and of arrival.

As mentioned earlier, C. G. Jung was certain he was guided by a daimon, Philemon, with whom, he claimed, he interacted both in his dreams and in his waking life. I'm not certain at all, but if I have an attendant spirit, his name must be 'Contrary.'

Contrary has never formally introduced himself to me,

but too many times in my life I've been a contrarian without a reason, almost by instinct. With counterculture dead and buried, this happens to be a healthy anti-propaganda approach, but sometimes it gets in the way of my best interest. The Greco-Roman philosopher Epictetus wrote: 'If a man opposes evident truths, it is not easy to find arguments by which we shall make him change his opinion. But this does not arise either from the man's strength or the teacher's weakness; for when the man, though he has been confuted, is hardened like a stone, how shall we then be able to deal with him by argument?'

Would this more or less conscious attitude of mine jeopardise a beautiful teacher/disciple relationship? Especially after I sent the following e-mail to Jaime?

What you say is wise and tested by years of experience at the highest levels. And yet, let me point out that at first Wang Hao [one of the world's top contemporary players] was shunned by the Chinese national team, and not allowed to play in it, because his style was considered unorthodox. But his revolutionary reverse backhand helped him to keep winning, and by dint of victories he became not only part of the team, but its leader. He certainly has revolutionised the style of penholders, and added a weapon to their repertoire.

I see that the 'unthinkable' is happening: Chinese rubbers adopting Japanese and/or European sponges; I see Butterfly, the most Japanese of all Japanese manufacturers, produce Chinese-inspired sticky rubbers with hard sponges. The 'hybridisation,' as you call it – a word I dislike because it reminds me of a mule – is already happening, and on a world scale. I prefer to call it 'cross-fertilization,' something that's occurring in all fields in this increasingly more interconnected world. I feel that in the future TT players will adopt cross-fertilised styles. It may not come from China, where there's too much academy, and academies, as you know, tend to get sclerotic.

So maybe it will be a European player who will train in China, and maybe also Korea and Japan.

When I execute certain 'cross-fertilised' shots, my grip changes. I don't even know if it's a shakehand grip any more. But I don't find them too difficult to execute.

I realise that the king of all table tennis strokes is the loop, no question about it. I embrace it, love it, and try to execute it also with the backhand, which is more difficult, so people neglect it – wrong. Then there are some little things whose efficacy I've tested over and over on lesser players. These aren't normally point-winners (well, they are, but only against non-entities); they help set up the next shot.

I do like style, and try to possess myself of all the conventional strokes to which I find natural to add some cross-fertilised ones. I could show you on the table why sometimes they're just more efficient and of faster execution, but that seems to irk you. That said, I use them rarely, so they don't deserve all this attention.

Thankfully there's constant evolution, or we should still be playing with hardbats, which I would not even bother to do because TT has become a game of spin. That's what has always attracted me to it, and if it weren't for spin, I wouldn't play at all.

Then there are aesthetics. Yesterday I beat this Indian guy who had a couple of nice tricks up his sleeve. But I beat him by using the 'wipers' tactics, making him run right and left and right again, you get the picture. It was god-awful tennis, yes, tennis, that's what it was, Euclidean and unsightly, and felt like cheap sex with a prostitute. That's a figure of speech since, unlike our unrepentant friend Emilio, I've never paid for sex, so I don't know how that feels, but I can imagine. In other words, I betrayed my TT aesthetics: if there are no colossal loads of spin, if non-Euclidean geometry doesn't take over, I shouldn't play at all. Winning is not the point.

I intend to keep developing the conventional strokes to the best of my abilities. Yes, my legs need to be energised, which means climbing stairs, walking, but also learning to move sideways. I have no problem moving forward and backward quickly, and I'm using the same legs. The reason for this may be found in fencing, eight years of it since I was six, which is all about back and forth with little lateral movement. So there are also habits inherited from other sports that need to be *unlearned*.

The purist's approach is right and wrong at the same time. If this weren't the case, if it weren't paradoxical, it wouldn't be table tennis. Purists create academies; academies create dogmas; dogmas create fossils. Technique, materials, ideas are in constant flux. Purity is as limiting as consistency.

In hindsight, this particular e-mail shows a few insights from a fresh perspective as well as a good dose of insolence. It would have put off a lesser teacher. Jaime probably just smiled, and put it down to my TT immaturity.

But there was also a difference in background. The artistic frame of mind favours creativity over consistency; innovation over convention; unpredictability over regularity; the exceptional over the normal. One wants to hear the word 'normal' only in reference to medical tests: 'Your results came back normal,' says the doctor, and we rejoice. But if we asked somebody, 'How's that new restaurant?' or 'that movie that just came out?' and got as a reply 'normal,' would we want to go eat at that restaurant or watch that movie?

Another point of friction was Jaime's insistence on that overrated concept of the modern world – statistics. When he was a professional player, he used to keep a log in which he recorded how many of his various strokes landed on the table, and how effectively, during each training session. For example, out of one hundred fore-hand loops in a row, how many landed *where* and *how* he wanted them to land, and how many did not. At the end of every week he would convert such figures into statistics so as to determine the consistency of his strokes. This image alone seems abhorrent to me, a player morphed into a hybrid between an automaton and an accountant. And that's because the most consequential things in our lives are, in fact, the *anti*-statistical occurrences we experience.

First and foremost, our very conception: that one sperm that, among an average of one hundred and ten million per ejaculation, wins the lottery by actually reaching the egg and fertilising it – bingo! We are all of us lottery winners for having being born when the odds against our conception were more than staggering, literally inconceivable: one to one hundred and ten million! What realistic chances did we stand? And yet, here we are.

The anti-statistical occurrence is the rare 'yes' we receive instead of the usual 'no' we expect and dread. Shortly after the horrific car accident in which I was involved and have mentioned earlier on, the police came to see me at the hospital. They barged into my room very early in the morning. I was in bed recovering from surgery with many broken bones, stitches on my brow arch and inside my lips, black and blue, just about everywhere, and having trouble breathing because of the broken ribs. The first thing one officer said was: 'Look here, we read all the statistics and see thousands of accidents: given the dynamics of yours, you really should be dead.'

And good morning to you too, Officer! I replied in my mind, but he was right: by cheating death I'd defied statistics. My being an exception, an anti-statistical occurrence was, in more antiquated language, a miracle. And Jaime was singing the praises of statistics!

I see now that it would have taken me a few more

months to understand what he meant. Regardless of what methods he employed, his search for perfect form had a higher meaning that I couldn't appreciate just yet, and of which I will write later on. And the whole point of standardising one's playing, possessing oneself of all the conventional strokes, and practising them over and over till they reach a very high percentage of consistency simply means *arriving at a threshold beyond which table tennis can become art*. Jaime, in fact, is an artist too and, as any true artist, also an artisan who knows that what comes first is technique. After all, the Greek word 'techni' translates in English as 'art.'

I had a long way to go, didn't realise it fully, and am grateful that Jaime proved so patient. All he said to me, probably biting his tongue, was, 'Why don't you play in another tournament?'

A club in Maryland was organising just then a team tournament divided into two categories: players below and above a rating of 1600. I signed up in the former category, and went on to recruit team members.

The first choice fell on the player I've presented in these pages as the nemesis of table tennis: Pedro, the Peruvian defensive empiricist with long pips. Why? Not only because consistency, as a general concept, remains hard to digest, but mainly because while he's a pest to play against, as a teammate he can be an asset.

The other choice fell on one-eyed Joe. He assured me that he'd wear a Jolly Roger patch on his blind eye for intimidation. Moreover, when we play as a team in a double, we speak French to each other, so the opponents can't understand what we're planning to do. The name we chose for our team was 'Absolute Beginners,' after David Bowie's song.

Two surprises awaited us: we were the only non-Chinese players; given that most of them hardly spoke English, our scheming in French would be redundant. And, they weren't exactly below 1600 players. In the first matches we were beaten by very accomplished players. I asked them about their rating and they said (as we eventually understood after various volunteers translated): 'Our rating is 1600, *cumulatively*.' Which means they had, say, two 2000-rated players and one absolute beginner; the latter never played but was officially a member of the team, and therefore brought down the average.

As if the game weren't complex enough in itself, sensory overload was grafted onto it. The place was crammed to bursting, not only by the participants, but by their raucous families – grannies, grandchildren and everyone in between – and assorted fans; there were photographers snapping and walking insouciantly between tables; electrical cords on the ground; it was chilly outdoors but an oven indoors; the floor quickly became covered in sweat, and therefore slippery; balls from other tables landed on one's table; little space between *and* behind tables hindered full movements; intense altercations flared up between different teams and their supporters; thirst was ever-present despite one's repeated attempts at quenching it, and hunger too, all the more since mouth-watering aromas of Chinese food brought by family members wafted in the air. Utter chaos, and yet refreshing: I felt as if I were a tiny component of a large dynamic system that behaved in a deterministic way and yet would yield unpredictable results, just like a hurricane – coincidentally the rubber of choice for most of the contenders. I realised then that this was going to be another initiation.

Every match we managed to win was considered an upset, as the usual bias was at work in this sort of extraterritorial Chinese enclave: western dudes playing TT? What?

The doubles were the most fun. Joe and I would routinely use under-the-table gestures. Before one serves, he shows his teammate what kind of spin he'll impress on the ball, which helps to predict how and where the opponent will return it. There are simple gestures for the basic spins, but the silent intercommunication quickly degenerated. When I served, I'd *also* extend my index and little fingers while holding the middle and ring fingers down with the thumb – the horns, a typical Italian gesture of various meanings, but none too flattering. When he served, he'd *also* give the opponents the middle finger, a more universal gesture. We didn't know where this frat-like mood had come from, but apart from making us laugh, it made us relax and play better.

We sobered up when Jaime arrived, accompanied by his son. Joe's girlfriend was present too, so we had a little support. We were then playing with a group whose overall strength more or less matched ours.

The look in Jaime's eyes spoke volumes. It seemed as if he tried to guide every ball we hit with his eyes. But for all his support and guidance – this time he didn't spare his advice – each team won two games, so we had to go for the fifth and final. We sensed that we were the strongest team, but Joe had more than his usual share of what he calls 'eye-balls' – balls that he misses or mis-hits because of his impaired vision. And the Jolly Roger patch on his blind eye wasn't really intimidating anybody.

We struggled to 10–9 in the last game. We had the match point, on Joe's serve. Jaime had given me some new advice before the fifth game: 'Don't be greedy.' From an all-out offensive player, this was startling. Another man bent on all-out attack, the mentioned military theorist von Clausewitz, wrote: 'It is even better to act quickly and err than to hesitate until the time of action is past.' So, I was caught between two waves. Going to deuce would have been psychologically in the opponents' favour: we should have won this match already.

Joe served, short, with backspin and a touch of sidespin. Their return was not very good but not very bad either. I didn't try to smash it, or even topspin it ('Don't be greedy,' Jaime had said), but safely chopped it back. The opponent did much of the same and Joe, pulling something out of his hat, made an unexpected and daring transition to topspin, with a forehand loop drive down the line, on their backhand. The opposing team was now in emergency mode: the player returned Joe's shot as best he could, but the ball was a little high over the net. 'Wait for the ball to settle,' Jaime had warned me. While taking aim I waited for the ball to be exactly where I wanted and placed a heavily topspinned backhand that they couldn't reach.

We had won, *¡Carajo!* as Jaime said. By now, many contenders had been eliminated, and some of them had lingered on, to watch. They, and other spectators, applauded us – us, the western dudes!

We went on to play several other matches. Pedro played his singles as if his life depended on it. He won several matches, but worked three times as hard for every point as a normal player would. Who knows, perhaps one day he'll gain enough confidence to become a metaphysician.

We ended in the middle, closer to the top than to the bottom. Considering that many players were well above the declared rating, this was a respectable result.

I lingered on to watch the semi-finals and finals. Two teams – and their respective retinues of rowdy fans and relatives – were then almost coming to blows. They needed a referee as badly as we need oxygen; so I volunteered. As the only western dude left in the place, they assumed I'd be impartial, and welcomed me. Everybody calmed down, and the matches enfolded in the proper way.

After the finals, all the players thanked me, and one of them, who spoke English uncharacteristically well, stayed on to chat with me. He was a physics teacher at a well-known high school in the area. Eventually the conversation turned to my impressions about the tournament, the first serious one in my life.

'How did you find it?' he asked.

'In one word, chaotic,' I replied.

'Well, it is. Sometimes I'm tempted to use TT

tournaments to introduce my students to the Theory of Chaos.'

My antennae were up. Seeing that I was interested, the teacher continued.

'When I first talk to my students about the Theory of Chaos I need to give them examples. To tell them that it's a mathematical sub-discipline that studies complex systems doesn't mean much. And I've learned that when I mention the behaviour of water boiling on a stove, or migratory patterns of birds, that doesn't mean much to them either. So once I told them about a tournament such as this one, except with more players and more tables yet. They got the picture.'

'So,' I said, 'a big table tennis tournament is a complex system?'

'Yes, it contains so many elements that move that computers are required to calculate all the various possibilities.'

'How's that?'

'It should be easy to predetermine the winning team by adding up the ratings of each team member. You must have noticed that we have two players rated higher than 1600, and one very low-rated player to bring down the average, who of course never plays. It'd be simple to add up the ratings of all *two* good players per team, and determine the winner simply by the highest score. But it doesn't work. That's why tournaments are fun, and chaotic: it's very difficult to predict the winner. And, of course, that's why Chaos Theory didn't emerge before the second half of the twentieth century: too many variables to calculate without computers. Just think about them.

'Let's say one player is slightly better than his opponent, as indicated by a slightly higher rating. But his style may be not compatible.' Which means that, despite a higher rating, the opponent has a style against which the better player typically struggles. 'Or, the opponent may get lucky and hit an unusual number of nets and edges.

'And then there are many other factors, like physical and mental condition; how much he's been training lately; what he ate that day, and when; if he's had an argument with his wife; how well he can see, as sometimes the lighting is poor, which tends to give an edge to younger players, and so on and on. Also, he may get hurt, not enough to leave the tournament, but enough not to play at one hundred per cent. So, even a single match's outcome can be unpredictable, let alone a team tournament with hundreds of players and sixty, seventy teams. But an educated guess based on a *distribution of probabilities*, that we can make, and that's what Chaos Theory teaches us.'

'Have you ever tried to map out a TT tournament this way?'

'Nah, and as far as I know nobody bothers to do this for a tournament at this level. There'd be a lot of computing involved. But I've been thinking about it, and I'm tempted. Factoring in the players' rating wouldn't be enough, obviously. That would be the determinists' approach, not the chaosticians', and we know that not even in regard to a TT tournament the determinists' approach works. I'd have to invent new ratings for each contender, such as the state of physical and mental form; compatibility between different players, and this alone would require many, many hours; and many other unusual variables. But one day I just might.'

We chatted some more, then I went home and collected my ideas.

The other reason for the recent birth of Chaos Theory, the teacher had added, is the Quantum Mechanical Revolution, and how it ended the deterministic era.

Quantum mechanics is the theory of the mechanics of atoms, molecules and other physical systems that are subject to the uncertainty principle. And in a nutshell the uncertainty principle, formulated by the German physicist Werner Heisenberg, says that the more one knows about where a particle is right now, the less one knows about how fast it's going and in what direction it's going. This applies also the other way around, which means that the more one knows about how fast it's going and in what direction it's going, the less one knows about where it is at present. In quantum physics the outcome of the most accurate measurement of a system isn't a fact; rather, it's shown by a probability distribution. This really changed the way we see the world, at least in the West.

Until the Quantum Mechanical Revolution the common belief was that things were directly caused by other things. Causality, in other words, was the force behind everything. Accordingly, what went up would come down, and if we could only tag every particle in the universe we could predict events from then onwards.

Systems of belief and governments were, and in many cases continue to be, founded on this rigid principle.

But the Theory of Chaos argues that nature works in patterns, which are caused by the sum of many complex components. Early Chaos theorists discovered that complex systems seem to run through a cycle, even though situations are seldom duplicated exactly. Complex systems, it transpired, often seek to settle in a specific situation. This situation may be static, which is called 'attractor,' or dynamic, which means in motion, which is called 'strange attractor.' All this has been sounding the death knell for determinism for decades.

Having always perceived determinism as the straitjacket of the mind, I find the Theory of Chaos liberating. Before we went our separate ways the teacher told me something that I jotted down right in front of him: 'Numbers can't fully represent reality because they're too accurate; they can't emulate the randomness that comes from the freedom that's the most fundamental principle of nature.'

The Theory of Chaos had always seemed a little nebulous and far-fetched to me. But table tennis had now clarified it, and made it compelling. It was exhilarating. Never mind the tournament and how we had performed: this was even more exciting. The universe seemed more beautiful yet, and I felt that it resonated, that day, with the intuition I'd had in my teens, when I would sit in the classroom staring appalled at the maths teacher with her nausea-inducing smugness in determinism and finiteness.

We think we can decide the outcome of our life through our deterministic efforts, but the dynamics of the complex systems we interact with negate this time and again. Embracing chaos is a saner approach, simply because it's more lifelike. Even in our own life, thinking in terms of 'probability distribution' is a more realistic and more flexible outlook than trying to predetermine a very precise goal. The latter can easily become a fixation, which at its direst can have disastrous consequences. We really should become 'chaosticians,' all the more so since we, in the western world, have been suppressing the concept of Chaos for centuries with our certainties and determinism, which have been proven misleading.

Table tennis kept working like a 'strange attractor' – taking me from equilibrium to equilibrium, but in constant motion. It kept showing me things I'd never have related to it. A celebration of Chaos seemed to be the latest entry. But for all our progress in beginning to appreciate the inner workings of chaotic nature, I was pleased to chance on a short story I'd read years ago by the Taoist philosopher Chuang Tzu, who lived in China in the fourth century BC.

'The Ruler of the Southern Ocean was Shû, the Ruler of the Northern Ocean was Hû, and the Ruler of the Centre was Chaos. Shû and Hû were continually meeting in the land of Chaos, who treated them very well. They consulted together how they might repay his kindness, and said, "Men all have seven orifices for the purpose of seeing, hearing, eating and breathing, while this (poor) Ruler alone has not one. Let us try and make them for him." Accordingly they dug one orifice in him every day; and at the end of seven days, Chaos died.'

12
Homo Ludens

When Jaime's wife says to her friends or colleagues that her husband, a distinguished economist in his early fifties, has gone to play ping-pong, they give her a commiserating look, and she knows what they're thinking: Ping-pong? Really? Is that the best lie he can come up with? Then he takes you for a moron – talk about adding insult to an injury.

It seems not only unlikely but altogether impossible that a busy professional rushes out of his office and go straight to a table tennis club. And once there, he gives it his all, sweating on average through three shirts per session. And he's only one of many successful professionals I've met who do just that.

Explaining reasons for cheating on their spouses would be easier: satisfying a repressed sexual urge; boredom with married life and the thrill of the illicit and clandestine; recapturing the flavour of their younger years, and so on. But such TT-playing professionals are neither bent on anything illicit nor satisfying a sexual urge, but rather responding to man's insatiable urge . . . to play. Emilio himself, while he certainly has never neglected his calling as a playboy, least of all now that he's pushing eighty, has likewise never neglected his urge to play.

I've philosophised our passion for table tennis by bringing into the equation Plato and Aristotle, metaphysics and empiricism, and various strains of the Perennial Philosophy; I've also psychologised it, resorting to Jung's concept of one's shadow. And while all of the above does stand, it's also true that some players aren't motivated, however unwittingly, by their shadow, nor are they consciously engaging in a metaphysical exploration or an initiatic voyage. They're drawn to the sport by an urge to play that is as irresistible as it's seemingly inexplicable.

We humans have been optimistically classified as *Homo sapiens*, knowing man. Judging from the history of our proud species, one would think that *Homo in-sapiens* might be more fitting, *un*knowing man. But the establishment, with the cultural canon it implements, works ever so assiduously at persuading us that evolution has been a great success, while the honest ones among us may suspect otherwise. Therefore one wonders if the official name that science has assigned to us, or the unofficial one, its opposite, should not be exchanged for something more descriptive and encouraging: *Homo ludens*, i.e., playing man.

The Dutch historian Johan Huizinga, author of the seminal book *Homo Ludens* on the role of playing in culture, wrote: 'Play is older than culture, for culture, however inadequately defined, always presupposes human society, and animals have not waited for man to teach them their playing.' Indeed, *Homo ludens*, playing man, free from the superimposed aspiration of being the brilliant result of an extraordinarily long evolution, would be able to delight in the most harmless and fun of all activities: play.

Such a simple notion, if properly conveyed, would give all schoolchildren reassurance that, once they grow into adults, the activity that's most dear to their heart – play – shall never have to cease. Like Huizinga, I too believe that it's possible for play to be the primary formative element in human culture.

But we're taught differently. It's as if the insatiable craving for play displayed by children were superseded by the equally insatiable craving for sex that, according to what we're told, will last until our senility, and then some. But it could be argued that repressing the very human urge to play has consequences as pernicious as repressing the very human sexual urge, as denounced by Freud when he was first exploring libido.

And yet, playing is frowned upon in the adult world. Think of the cautionary tale *The Adventures of Pinocchio*. In it, the fictional location The Land of Toys, renamed in the Disney film adaptation Pleasure Island, serves as a haven for wayward boys, allowing them to act as they please and play all they want without any recrimination. However, the truer and more sinister purpose of Pleasure Island is eventually revealed as it begins physically to transform the boys into donkeys. The message here is straightforward: boys and girls, be wary of play – it will turn you into donkeys!

The Greek myth of the *puer aeternus*, the eternal child, has been co-opted so as to discredit adults who are as keen on playing as when they were children. Analytical psychology uses as an example of the eternal child *The Little Prince*, by the French writer Antoine de Saint-Exupéry, a story so well loved by the whole world, indeed one of the best-selling books of all time, that one wonders if being a *puer æternus* could be all that bad?

It seems to me that if mankind were allowed to dedicate much more time to playing, there would be less hostility in the world, and probably fewer wars. And table tennis, both enormously popular and thoroughly cosmopolitan, points precisely in this direction.

Looking at us players waiting for our turn around a table, I travel back in time by decades, and detect the same eagerness I felt back in that summer camp in the Dolomites, when I was little more than a child. What has changed? So much, and at the same time, so little. Grown men behave exactly like children – and, in this context, it's refreshing. This calls to mind the alchemical motive of *ludus puerorum*, child's play. Esoteric writings on alchemy often state that once the primitive materials of the philosopher's stone have been obtained, the rest of the Great Work is a simple labour, or 'child's play.' The playing child is probably linked with the alchemical idea of regeneration. The end result is metaphysical, for both the child and the adult player. The only difference is that while the child is inherently wise – his wisdom soon to be spoiled by schooling of a certain type – for the adult such wisdom is a return to a better state.

But the adult's urge to play is actively repressed. Instead of playing, we're 'entertained,' which is not only allowed but heavily promoted. The entertainment industry is huge, and rather than participating we're made to sit and watch, or listen. Professional athletes and musicians 'play;' a comedy or drama at the theatre is a 'play;' playing, in short, is always evoked, but we adults are supposed only to witness it as passive spectators, and derive all our enjoyment from that. Why? Videogames have shown to the entertainment industry the willingness people have to *participate* in a game. Ask any child if he or she would rather watch their favourite sport or play it, and she or he will always say, 'Play it!'

Huizinga wrote: 'The *fun* of playing resists all analysis, all logical interpretation.' He added: 'Here, then, we have the first characteristic of play: that it is free, is in fact freedom. A second characteristic is closely connected with this, namely, that play is not "ordinary" or "real" life. It is rather a stepping out of "real" life into a temporary sphere of activity with a disposition all of its own.'

The contemporary intelligentsia, which has been having a dalliance with scepticism for decades, may be opposed to the role of play for yet another reason. The French poet and philosopher Paul Valéry wrote: 'No scepticism is possible where the rules of a game are concerned, for the principle underlying them is an unshakable truth.' The play-world rests on absolutes; it is a world apart, at the antipodes, in fact, of our 'real' world, built on the shaky foundations of relativism.

One Sunday afternoon my ongoing exploration of the

play-world and the World of Forms took me to the Chinese club. There were three goodish Chinese players, one of them the maths professor I knew from my early attempts at the community centre close to home. Since those days the gap between us had closed. The place in Chantilly was cold (I never really broke a sweat), the cheap training balls didn't bounce anything like the three-star ones I'm used to, and the tables were also different from the ones at my club, and not as good. So I played inconsistently; I won the occasional game, but not an entire match. Still, the three Chinese had a different opinion of me by the time we were done playing. Then came Mofi, an Iraqi with a peculiar personal history.

Born in Baghdad, Mofi was a player in the Iraqi national water polo team; then went to study mechanical engineering in Prague; moved on to Stockholm, eventually settling there and getting married before coming to the States. Here he owns a restaurant called Tigris in honour of his motherland. Every time I go to eat there with Tano, our firstborn son, he can't help mocking me, having played with me many times. He thinks of himself as a great player. Recently he even had the nerve to say that I'm too old to beat him – and what is he? Sixty-five?

Anyway, we warmed up and played a match. Once more I was impatient, because I quickly realised that now *I* was the superior player, and was eager to get it over with. So, naturally, he won, 3–0.

Whenever I missed a serve, he'd say, 'Thank you!' whenever I got upset at my own mistake, he'd say, 'Don't get discouraged!' My blood was boiling. With all that, he won barely, 11–9; then at the advantages; then 11–9 again. And there was another detail: I noticed that Mofi was using always the same ball, though in that club there are balls everywhere on the floor and you normally pick up the closest one. As soon as I realised that, I made it a point to change the ball whenever I could. It made no difference to me – they were all of inferior quality. But the detail was telling: he was trying to eke out every small advantage: the same ball would produce the same bounces, thus lessening the difficulty of having to adjust to slightly different bounces all the time.

We played a second match. By now we were fully immersed in what Huizinga calls 'a world apart.' I said to myself: Guido, be patient. You're the better player; you've got a repertoire that he can't even dream of; you've got strategy; he's the dog, you're the wolf.

What was that? Where did that intrusion from the world of the novelist Jack London come from? Besides, isn't White Fang a *dog*? But such is the nature of any game: so dead serious, when observed from the outside it seems preposterous.

We began. Mofi is essentially a defensive player with tremendous control and a predilection for the backhand, which makes him play in the centre of the table. He chops a lot and makes the best of what he can do, because as far as mobility is concerned, he's a bit 'nailed' to the floor, as Jaime would put it.

There'd be an exchange of chops, usually backhand, and then I'd topspin the ball, and do in essence what I wanted with it. I scored after a series of loops, from either forehand or backhand, or mixed; or with loop-kills; or with placement; or with flat smashes; or even with chops, and serves. I didn't play it safe, I used my whole repertoire, including loop-kills from out of position to his left when he was expecting them to his right. In short, I won soundly: 11–6; 11–6; 11–5.

Now he was silent; he had no idea what to do. His every attempt at topspinning my chops ended in the net. When I'd open the play and invite the topspin exchanges, he wouldn't know how to cope with either my placement or my constant variations in the topspin itself. In other words: *I* was in control, and *he* looked like an old man chasing after balls he couldn't realistically hope to reach.

My satisfaction was profound. This was a former professional athlete, and still very much a jock. People like me don't beat people like him in sports. He'd no longer mock me, and I'd won with difficult shots and a good variety of them in contrast to his asinine play. The win instilled self-confidence, but instant regret, too: the time of discounts and freebies at his restaurant was probably over.

In fact, I've recently gone back to his restaurant with Jaime and another Dominican superior player, Jose, and Mofi has offered us all a sumptuous meal. I'm bound to correct myself: more than a jock, he is a true sportsman.

On a trip to New York City shortly after that, I was delighted to go for the first time to a veritable Land of Toys, or Pleasure Island, smack in the heart of Manhattan: the club SPiN, with seventeen ping-pong tables, a full bar, restaurant, etc., open all the way to four in the morning. And what is more, after midnight one can play for free. And shortly after midnight I went there for the first time, to find a mixed crowd: good and not-so-good players, loiterers, models, assorted weirdoes, you name it.

My first opponent is a talented Asian, a penholder. We warm up and quickly enter the 'play-world.' We're playing intensely, and a little crowd gathers around our table. Among them, I catch a glimpse of Abdul, of all people, the Egyptian with the 'sick' daughter. I don't know why that should bother me so much, but I start throwing away points, and quickly lose the match.

After the incident at the tournament I'd come across Abdul from time to time in other clubs, but always steered clear of him. I'd also heard him say that he'd become too good for our club.

I say hello to him, and leave the table.

He follows me.

Oh no, I think. I see somebody waiting at another table, alone, and ask her if she wants to play. I'm on.

Abdul stops by, waiting.

I play with Lisa, a young woman from Brooklyn as it turns out. I play poorly, let her win the first game, barely win the second and the same goes for the third. More than playing I'm toying with her, unconcerned by the outcome. In effect, I don't want the match to end. Completely relaxed, I don't believe I'm bending my legs at all; terrible form. Abdul is watching all along and paying his typical false compliments to both Lisa and me. It's the way he gets when he pays compliments: so condescending, false and sycophantic at the same time – it must be a special talent of his.

Now it's Abdul's turn. He's been waiting for this, though my poor performance with Lisa must have sown doubts. Is this guy really worth my time? he must be thinking. Maybe he avoids me because he knows that he'll lose.

When I first arrived at the club in Arlington, he was the king there, or pimp-master, as our son Pietro would have it. He wore a bandanna on his bald head and thought the world of himself. The spectacle then was impressive: the smugness so explicit was incongruously blended with his (falsely) courteous ways.

Back to SPiN, New York. We start playing, and I'm equally relaxed with him, still deciding whether or not I want to be engaged at all. Perhaps I'm bending my legs a little, but nothing compared to my posture and concentration when I was playing Mofi only days before.

Still, as I am (kind of) playing with Abdul, I realise that my minimum effort is giving him trouble. A defensive player who speculates on the opponent's mistakes expects to be attacked, but attacking I'm not. So, with little physical effort, I take the first game, a very close 11–9. This gives him the impression that we really are just about equal, which must still be unnerving to him, because from the heights of his hubris he had just passed judgement anew on me and – how could he lose, however closely?

In the second game I make more of an effort, and treat him to some of my repertoire. Once more I have the distinct feeling that, like Mofi, he's a one-trick pony. The more I play, the more I realise how ignorant of the game he really is despite years of practice and miles of hubris. I serve, he puts it in the net. I repeat the same serve, or so he thinks, he sends it out, long – doesn't understand when I'm backspinning or topspinning. I go for an over-the-table forehand loop-kill, he dives to his right, I place it down the line to his left. I seem to be topspinning with my backhand, but I'm only pretending and in fact hitting it flat, he closes the racket too much to counter the perceived topspin, and puts it in the net. I make him run from left to right a few times, but then I keep insisting on his right side till, thanks to a hooked topspin, he can no longer reach the ball. I need no sabre to dispatch him: the foil is enough. A comfortable 11–6, in both the second and the third games.

I hasten to add that I hit neither nets nor edges, behave gentlemanly, even praise his occasional good shot. At first he was praising mine too, but then, somehow, he stopped.

Both he and Mofi play what I call 'parasitic' table tennis. These are those players who cling indefinitely to their 'shortcuts,' which will grant them many wins, to be sure, but past a certain ranking, no more. Had Abdul been trying to improve instead of playing his cheap, homespun style, he should be better than I am, since he's been at it for so much longer.

Jaime would have probably wanted me to use the sabre instead of the foil, but that would have been unnecessary. I resorted to technique and finesse – everything that Abdul has been working so hard at depriving his style of.

After the match we shook hands and I stepped aside. But the expression on Abdul's face – *that* spoke volumes.

This is the same man who, in order to get rid of me at the tournament, had had no qualms about inventing that his little daughter was at home lying on her deathbed. I could read in his eyes what he was thinking: I've been at this for decades, in fact I left the club in Arlington because I was too good for it, and now this nobody can give me a lesson by playing so nonchalantly, and ridicule me?

The blindness of his hubris must have dawned on him then – smug? In what? His own mediocrity? Oh well . . . Pop! Goes the weasel!

13
Pilgrimage to the Holy Land

I was sitting in a brand-new Airbus that sported unusually young and good-looking flight attendants. Beside me sat my wife. It had been her idea, a very good one as usual.

During a trip to Vancouver we'd fallen in love with British Columbia. Pleasant surprises awaited us everywhere we went. One of them was the city's large Chinese population. We went to the Golden Village in the suburb of Richmond – which has received the heaviest immigration from China in recent years – to have an authentic meal, and happened to pick up some free magazines. In one of them my wife found an irresistible deal for a trip to China. And here we were, finally 'crossing the great water,' as the I Ching puts it, on a flight to Beijing. A *very* long flight.

My fascination with table tennis had begun with the mythical Orient – the Japanese racket so deftly handled by that boy high up in the Dolomites. Decades later my passion had grown under the influence of Chinese players and equipment. 'Crossing the great water' seemed to make sense. I'd been attracted to various aspects of Chinese culture for years, and finally going there would be a pilgrimage to the Holy Land, and not only of table tennis. For some weeks before leaving I'd been jotting down thoughts about what struck me as major differences between the Chinese and western cultures, and was now rereading them.

The Chinese never developed an alphabet, but rather ideograms, or Sinograms, or, better yet, Han characters. The Kangxi Dictionary contains the astonishing number of 47,035 characters. Compared to the twenty-four letters of the Greek alphabet, the twenty-three of Classical Latin and the thirty of the German alphabet, it's evident that writing and reading in Mandarin is an effort, which explains the emphasis placed by Chinese culture on calligraphy. In stark contrast, I remember that in my elementary school it was perceived that the children with the fine handwriting were the dumb ones, whereas the clever ones couldn't be bothered by handwriting per se, as long as it was legible.

Ancient Greek, Latin and German have been used by most of the greatest philosophers of the western tradition, with Latin being the lingua franca of European scholars for centuries. Intellectuals would inevitably be tempted to play around with words. For example, by arranging and rearranging a mere thirty letters, the rationalist, specu-lative and idealist German philosopher Hegel amassed hundreds of thousands of words in formidable books of immense breadth and complexity that revolutionised nineteenth-century European philosophy. In his view, spirit, concept and theory had supremacy over all. Reality was a product of theory. In a famous incident, a student of his dared to say: 'Professor, your theory is perfect, but it doesn't correspond to reality.'

'Then,' thundered the irate philosopher, 'too bad for reality!'

At 36,000 feet of elevation, the supreme folly of this hit me like a table tennis smash in the eye. It was as if Hegel had said, 'My brilliant philosophical system can't be bothered by such trivial matters. No correspondence to reality? Who cares, to hell with reality!'

But it's precisely this steadfast belief in abstract concepts that don't relate to reality that has had terrible consequences for humanity. In a court of law, denying evidence is a crime. In western philosophy, it seems to be perfectly permissible.

Chinese philosophy pales in comparison to the enormous western collection of mental acrobatics, and that seems inevitable, considering the unwieldiness of their script. But, judging from the results of western philosophising, isn't that a blessing in disguise?

Lao Tzu is a sage of ancient China and a key figure in Taoism. Whether he actually lived or is a legendary figure remains to be established, but he's considered to be the author of the *Tao Te Ching*, a fundamental book in both philosophical Taoism and Chinese religion. In it is the assertion: 'Banish wisdom, discard knowledge, / and the people shall profit a hundredfold.'

Excluding Plato and all Neoplatonic schools, this is how from 'love of Sophia,' or of wisdom, literally philosophy, has degenerated into 'love of sophistry' – precisely the type of 'wisdom' and 'knowledge' that Lao Tzu urges us to discard. I've long suspected that the western effortlessness in creating and amassing words has resulted in seriously overrated verbiage.

I could see at last that it was table tennis, once more, that had driven this conclusion home. It's no coincidence that the Chinese, along with players from other Asian countries, would be the best in the world. I'd been learning firsthand how incredibly complex table tennis can be. The higher the level of play, the more complex it becomes. But then it's played at such a pace, there's hardly enough time to 'read' all the spins. The top players in the world have reached a threshold beyond which they have 'discarded all knowledge,' brought to a standstill all distracting thoughts, quieted all moods and emotions, stopped all discursive thinking so as to *concentrate*, from the Latin *com-* 'together, with' and *centrum* 'centre.'

At such levels, table tennis becomes a wordless, pure meditation. There's no more reading, thinking, intellectual processing. Alphabets, syntax, mental acrobatics, no matter how quick, couldn't cope. Not surprisingly, several of the European top players have trained in China, too.

A fine-looking flight attendant – her face suffused with lunar pallor – called me back to more immediate concerns. With a smile, she asked: 'What type of breakfast would you like? Western or Chinese?'

'Chinese, of course!' I replied enthusiastically, and added in my mind, What else?

She gracefully handed over an object wrapped in tinfoil

while my wife looked on and smiled, amused. Other passengers were unwrapping theirs, so I imitated them.

I was holding in my hands something similar to an egg in shape, but of a green/brown colour with a very wrinkled surface. I had no idea what to do with it. Other passengers began to bite theirs, so I did too.

The taste was . . . not of this world, nothing I'd eat under normal circumstances. But I was hungry and, even more, enthusiastic; I wanted to take the plunge into Chinese culture and started, as it happened, with a rank seaweed-encrusted hard-boiled egg with overtones of rot and something else that escaped me.

Other unusual breakfast items were offered but, somehow, I passed on them and went back to my notes. What greeted me then was a milestone in the more recent history of western philosophy: the *Tractatus Logico-Philosophicus*, a logical-philosophical treatise by the revered Austrian thinker Ludwig Wittgenstein.

In compiling my notes before leaving I'd consulted my old copy of the *Tractatus*. It was water-stained as, along with other books in my library, it had survived not entirely unscathed the destructive force of Hurricane Andrew, which hit Miami in 1992. This was a cherished book from my younger years, one in which, I'd believed, much wisdom had been distilled. And such a slim book, made up by a collection of numbered aphorisms, is considered to this day among the five most influential philosophical works of the twentieth century. Its penultimate aphorism reads: 'My propositions are elucidatory in this way: he who understands me finally recognises them as senseless, when he has climbed out through them, on them, over them. (He must so to speak throw away the ladder, after he has climbed up on it.) He must transcend these propositions, and then he will see the world aright.'

Wittgenstein borrows an analogy from Arthur Schopenhauer, a nineteenth-century German philosopher, and compares his own book to a ladder that must be thrown away after one has climbed it. That's because through the philosophy of the book one must realise the utter *meaninglessness* of philosophy. Well, that will set the world aright, all right!

Once more Lao Tzu's exhortation echoed in my mind: 'Banish wisdom, discard knowledge, / and the people shall profit a hundredfold.'

A decade later, a Viennese philosopher and logician, Rudolf Carnap, wrote that 'Wittgenstein has clearly formulated the proud thesis of omnipotence of rational science.' And then, in the book *Philosophy and Logical Syntax*, Carnap used the concept of verifiability to reject metaphysics altogether.

So there it was: centuries and centuries of philosophical evolution had brought mankind triumphantly to this: the rejection of both philosophy *and* metaphysics. Some of the allegedly most brilliant minds in Europe had worked assiduously at the annihilation of the love of wisdom, and supplanted it with sophistry. With their blessing, the twentieth century could be, at long last, spiritually bankrupt – as, by and large, it *has* been in the western world.

But early on in the twenty-first century, at 36,000 feet above our spinning Planet Earth, all this seemed tragicomically misguided. Not only Taoism, but also Zen, Sufism, the mystery religions, eastern and western esotericism, mysticism of different traditions – all have shown and continue to show us that the Perennial Philosophy is just that: perennial. Western theoretic philosophy, on the other hand, seems to have degenerated into sophistry and verbiage.

At the airport we were met by our tour guide. 'Where are the other travellers?' we asked.

'Oh, they've all cancelled.'

For the whole journey, we were told, we'd have a van with a chauffeur and a guide/interpreter at our exclusive disposal. An unforeseen private tour everywhere, in other words. It was an auspicious beginning.

For two weeks we saw and experienced all we could. I had a phrasebook with me, and for fun I'd ask the driver and the guide to guess what I was telling them in Mandarin, a tonal language that's particularly difficult to pronounce for westerners. At times I was understandable; when I wasn't, my pronunciation was apparently so hilarious that the driver, laughing hysterically, would have to pull over lest he lose control. We soon realised that the Chinese are, in general, quick to laugh, so I emphasised whatever latently comical situation presented itself with a lot of laughter as a result.

The country struck us as energetic and energising, shrouded in pollution under permanently grey skies, unfortunately, but full of promise. The people seemed happy, and everywhere we went we found them to be welcoming and affable. It was nice to be caught in this general euphoria.

Feng shui is alive and well and many things, we were told, bring good luck, others bad. For example, we were encouraged by everyone we met to go to the Great Wall: merely touching it couldn't fail to bring us good luck. Of course we did, and whether it brought us good luck or not, well, it's a matter of opinion, though from a strictly table tennis perspective, you'll be able to judge for yourself by the time you've finished this book. One way or the other, we were in the midst of what seemed a superstitious society, and it was a pleasant surprise.

The Temple of Heaven in Beijing – regarded as a Taoist temple even if Heaven-worship predates Taoism – was crowded, and not just by tourists. There were worshippers, many of them. Every temple we visited in China, in every city, teemed with worshippers burning incense, praying, meditating. Now, China isn't India. One doesn't strike up a philosophical conversation just about anywhere, be it with a beggar or with a guru. In fact, we tend to think of China as a country of very pragmatic people with a keen sense of commerce and an immense capacity for work. There was plenty of that too, to be sure, but nothing had prepared us for a spiritual people.

Ever a lover of botany, I noticed mostly teenage trees, and all native to China. For a moment I wondered, guilt-stricken, if tens of millions of table tennis rackets had contributed to the felling of all mature trees?

The food situation was also odd. The Chinese claim that they eat just about anything, and the menus we saw attested to this: dogs, donkeys, monkeys, snakes, starfish, insects, very peculiar animal parts, and so on. And yet, entire food groups are missing. Bread and its derivates aren't available; there's no trace of milk, yogurt, cheese, cream, butter, ice cream and creamy sauces. Desserts aren't their prerogative, neither is wine, which they do produce, but as a curiosity. Also conspicuously absent are the foods from the 'new world': tomato, potato, corn, chocolate, vanilla. They're still to be incorporated in their cuisine. The absence of tomato and potato is particularly intriguing since China, as it turns out, is the world's top producer of both. What on earth do they do with fifty million tons of tomatoes and eighty million tons of potatoes? Next time you buy a can of Italian peeled tomatoes or a bag of Idaho potatoes, make sure you read the fine print.

We saw people of all ages play table tennis in public parks, hundreds of tables made of concrete next to one another. One afternoon my wife treated me to a detour. A Chinese member of the club back in the States had told me about a legendary street behind the 'Sports Bureau' full of TT shops. 'Jeff' – that's how he wants to be called by westerners – can tell a player's blood type just by looking at the way he plays. He never misses. Uncanny. Anyway, our guide found the street, which teemed with table tennis shops.

Some were the official showplaces of giant manufacturers, be they Chinese, Japanese or European; others sold all sorts of intriguing brands. In the DHS shop I bought a certain blade and two rubbers, and two very attentive female employees assembled the racket right in front of us.

What I had done at home many times in a rather improvised way occasionally mixed with inadvertent slapstick, they approached as a ritual. Dividing the different tasks between the two of them, they applied the glue on the blade and the rubbers. Then, using small and quiet blow-dryers, they hastened the drying of the glue on both surfaces. The rubber, once stuck onto the blade, was cut to size with immaculate precision, as was the other one. The assembling of the racket was in itself a feat of technical prowess. It had taken them no more than five minutes.

We walked down the street and explored each shop. In one of them there was a match in progress between two young players, male and female. We asked with sign language if we could watch, and the shopkeeper welcomed us in.

We learned later from our guide, who talked to the shopkeeper, that the two players were team members in the selection from their province. I had never witnessed play of this level only ten feet away from me. It was a thorough display of good form, no, splendid, sublime, Platonic form. Their rallies seemed choreographed, but weren't, as this was a real practice match, not an exhibition. They employed only correct strokes, in the right order according to the situation at hand; the structure of their playing was clearly thought out, with both balance and rhythm being an integral part of it. Their concentration was exceptional. I could tell that they were rapt in a realm above ours. While they played, they conversed, or rather held discourse, in the World of Forms. When an ambulance careened down the street, its siren screeching, neither player seemed to notice. From the outside, it looked like a performing trance. But, having myself glimpsed some occasional insights into what such players were seeing, I knew it was something well above a trance.

The match came to an end; who won doesn't matter. It took the contenders a while before they would say a word. Not out of physical exertion, although, obviously, they were tired. No, they had to scale down and, from the World of Forms, descend back into ours. Eventually they did, and, with our guide acting as interpreter, proved affable. I congratulated them warmly and then asked for tips, about both equipment and certain strokes. Among other things, they both strangely recommended us to visit the Forbidden City.

The enormous imperial palace and compound in the middle of Beijing was a daunting prospect. In the oppressive summer heat, it felt as though we could have walked in it for days. The architecture and artistic decorations were to say the least impressive, though I'm sure that much was lost on us due to our lack of specific knowledge. But why had the provincial team members told us to come here? What did it have to do with table tennis?

Eventually our guide led us through a maze of small streets in what looked like a small village within the Forbidden City. In it there were some shops. He escorted us into one, saying: 'This is a calligraphy shop. The nephew of Aisin-Gioro Puyi, the last Emperor, is a calligrapher. He works here.'

Calligraphy? I thought. Oh dear . . . Nine years before I'd seen an exhibit in a museum in Washington, DC, about Chinese calligraphy. It was my wife who insisted that we go there since I wasn't interested. She enjoyed the exhibit while I didn't get it at all. She bought a calligraphy kit and has since practised at home; I, on the other hand, wrote on an album in which visitors were asked to pen down their comments: 'Long live the Roman alphabet!' It seemed to me that in its extreme concision and practicality it had served and was still serving western civilisation very well.

So, what was I doing in a calligraphy shop? Moreover, it looked like a classic tourist trap, one to which all western tourists, and many Chinese ones too, would be taken by their guides to get a commission on whatever they'd buy. Still, this was the last Emperor's nephew, an aged and skilled calligrapher; we were in the heart of the Forbidden City, the epicentre of Chinese power for centuries; the least I could do was show respect.

The calligrapher was delivering a speech; sitting beside him, an interpreter was translating it into English. The first words we heard were: 'Competency in a particular style requires many years of practice. Correct strokes, stroke order, character structure, balance, rhythm are essential in calligraphy.'

I did a double take; the same words could have been said about table tennis. Was that why the advanced players had insisted that we come here? Did they know that at the end of our visit we would invariably be taken to the calligraphy shop? Probably, since they too, coming from the provinces, might have had the same experience, and recently.

It was clear that the aged calligrapher was giving only a very succinct history of calligraphy, a subject on which, I could see around us, hundreds of books have been written.

There's a debate about whether East-Asian calligraphy is a discipline or an art, as it may well be both. Chinese calligraphy masters in each dynasty enriched the styles and structures of the characters with their insight, emotion and artistic sensibility. Chinese masters consider calligraphy a highly disciplined mental exercise that coordinates body and soul, not only so as to choose the best possible way to express the content, but also for one's physical and spiritual well-being and enlightenment.

The old master then proceeded to demonstrate how a calligrapher operates. In his deliberate and elegant brushstrokes even I could detect decades of dedicated training and a degree of balance a trapeze artist would envy. I also thought I sensed the man's instant departure from our realm to reach the World of Forms. And then it finally hit me.

Sometimes a revelation, once revealed, seems perfectly obvious. But I suppose I had to go all the way to China to come to grips with this particular one while my wife, given her pre-existing interest in Chinese calligraphy, had been open to it all along. We were being shown by the old and very skilful master how essential each stroke of the brush is. I could easily imagine the man's training, beginning in his childhood.

Every child in China has to learn calligraphy, whether or not later on in life he or she will become a professional calligrapher. From their earliest years, they're implicitly taught to revere form because it is of the essence. And much as they train their hand at calligraphy, so do they train it at table tennis, this most popular of sports. In this, too, they find a strict discipline, and precise movements and strokes to learn and replicate until they make them their own. To this training they also submit readily. It's obvious even to such young minds that with no training there would be no skill.

Conversely, increasingly less time is spent in US schools to teach the children to write in cursive (in our immensely simpler approach to the written word). Ball-and-stick manuscript writing is more popular. Smartphones and computers improve the children's typing skills, but their penmanship is, inevitably, terrible.

Schools in the western world seldom if ever teach the students to use their hands. The emphasis is overwhelmingly on the intellectual sphere. Most young men and women graduate from universities without having a clue how to use their hands.

In East-Asian countries, once the students have come of age, some will become professional calligraphers, others professional table tennis players – and those who won't become either, the vast majority of them, will still have been given great tools of self-growth and self-knowledge. Lao Tzu wrote: 'Knowing others is intelligence; / knowing yourself is true wisdom.' One of education's main goals should remain self-knowledge. This is no foreign concept, but it rather belongs to the Perennial Philosophy; in ancient Greece, for example, the famous aphorism 'Know thyself' was inscribed in the forecourt at the Temple of Apollo in Delphi.

Chinese professional calligraphers will cultivate their every stroke of the brush; professional table tennis players, their every stroke of the racket. But advanced table tennis players do not just hit the ball – they *brush* it. For every *brushstroke* in calligraphy there is a *brushed stroke* in table tennis. It's no wonder, then, that so much of the best table tennis in the world is to be found in East-Asian countries, in all of which calligraphy is revered as the purest of arts.

And it's here that the typical western distinction between form and content is lost. For the East-Asian calligrapher as well as for the table tennis player, form is not only of the essence; form *is* the essence. This was my belated revelation, brought to light by table tennis in conjunction with East-Asian calligraphy: *form is the essence.*

In the western world even our vocabulary has devalued and trivialised the word 'form.' There's the expression – Latin but still used in English – 'pro forma,' which is something done merely for the sake of (vacuous) form, but perceived as not vital. A 'formality' can mean as little as a requirement of custom or etiquette. And a 'conformist' is a person who uncritically conforms to the customs, rules or styles of a group. I felt angry at myself for having been so blind. My contrarian nature had failed me; I *had* bought into the propaganda of the modern western world; I *had* thought little if anything of form. Jaime, on the other hand, had always striven towards perfect form because *form is the essence.*

But isn't this what Plato taught us, too? In the separation between our mundane world of sense-perception and the World of Forms lies the difference between a life in captivity and one in the presence of the spiritual Absolute. It was finally clear to me that in China and in the rest of Eastern Asia both calligraphers and table tennis players are on the same quest for pure form.

So, here I was: the same man who nine years before had mocked and dismissed Chinese calligraphy as unwieldy, and exalted, by contrast, the practicality of the Roman alphabet, was now talking to the old calligrapher, and thanking him warmly for his wisdom. Is contradiction a good sign? I think so. Aristotle, who in his *Metaphysics* invented also the principle of contradiction, finding me in violation of one of his three classic laws of thought would disagree vehemently – but what else is new?

The two players from the provincial team had given me also some more straightforward advice on equipment. After the ITTF's ban on speed glue, they had said, manufacturers have come up with 'pre-tuned' rubbers that have permanent speed-glue effect. The rubbers, I was told, are treated in a fume box expanded with nitrous oxide, then exposed to a non-VOC (volatile organic compounds) gas that locks the expansion in place. And one of such new rubbers I had just bought – the Skyline 3 NEO. It was appropriate that DHS, which is headquartered in Shanghai, would name its best (in my view) rubber by taking its cue from the city's impressive skyline.

In overwhelming Shanghai we visited a large DHS shop. Our guide there had a nice attitude but spoke very little English, and the people in the shop none at all. But they took me straight to the back. I entered a huge warehouse with shelves heaped with hundreds, thousands of rubbers. I was in heaven, hadn't been this excited in years. My wife said that I looked like a child in a huge toy store, and took pictures.

In the end an energetic saleswoman persuaded me to

buy Wang Hao's very blade – Hurricane Hao – which he himself, my favourite player in the world, has developed and plays with – a dainty and light wooden wonder with a huge 'sweet spot.' I also bought a nice variety of rubbers, but had the pre-tuned Skyline 3 NEO glued onto this blade, too.

Just thinking back about this makes me smile, but there's another reason for that: the simple transaction took almost two hours. I had very few words in Mandarin, and stretched them well beyond their limits. They would reply in Mandarin and, rather than say nothing, which I thought would be rude, I'd repeat what they'd said like a parrot. That made them explode in uproarious laughter. No wonder! As far as I knew, I could have been repeating: 'Why does he even bother, pathetic inept westerner?' But probably not; they were just trying to talk to me, but all I could do was repeat their words, and not that well either. Everybody in the shop laughed so much, by the time we finally left there were tears in their eyes and streaking down their cheeks. For different reasons, it'd been a memorable visit for all involved. And now I was itching to try out my new equipment.

14

Can the Stars Be Outwitted?

Towards the end of our journey my wife and I were wondering if this could still be the China of Taoism and of the I Ching with its baffling oracles and its superior man or woman? The image we in the West have of China is one of an economic giant working hard to usurp the US of its primacy. And while we had seen some of its tremendous economic growth – where are the bicycles? Cars were everywhere – the country as a whole struck us as being much more concerned than we westerners are with things that don't meet the eye. There's an almost palpable spiritual dimension, there, that is lacking in the West, but then, as my wife said when I shared my views with her, 'Any place is more spiritual than the West.'

We realised by then that feng shui, for example, is very present in people's minds, and much more felt than it could be in the West, where it's a fad. There would be a western equivalent of sorts, the *genius loci* of the ancient Romans, which was the guardian, or genie, of a place as well as the character or atmosphere of such a place in reference to the impressions that it made on the mind. But who remembers that nowadays? On the other hand in China people believe to this day that following the criteria of feng shui – based on both astronomy and geography, the Tao of Heaven and Earth – helps one receive positive 'Qi,' roughly translated as energy flow.

And the I Ching, whether used as a divination system or a philosophical book, contains teachings that, incredibly, are still put to use, five thousand years after its creation.

In one of the many museums we visited we chanced on a sumptuous collection of Song Dynasty ceramics. Until then I'd thought of Chinese decorative arts as Chinoiserie, a recurring theme in European artistic styles since the seventeenth century. 'Orientalisation' was characterised by intricate patterns and a very extensive use of motifs instantly identifiable to the western eye as Chinese. To this day when a westerner thinks of Chinese porcelain and decorative arts in general that's what comes to mind. But the Song Dynasty ceramics, dating back to 960–1279, are nothing of that sort. By comparison to what preceded them and what was to follow, the shapes of Song Dynasty ceramics are of a sublime simplicity, concentrating on the meditative qualities of form. The glazes, too, tend to be monochromatic and subtle, an integral part of the form they cover, with a great depth of colour and texture. These deceptively simple ceramics are an ode to understatement and economy of expression. It's a deliberately minimalistic approach, since the artists possessed all the skills to produce something very elaborate.

The same sublime simplicity can be found in table tennis of the highest level. More than half of what world-class players do in their matches goes unnoticed by the general public. Their 'heroic' loops are self-evident, but the work they put into neutralising – or compensating for – incoming spin is lost on the casual viewer, as is their footwork, which is so seamless that it appears effortless. A game of tremendous complexity is distilled into the sublime simplicity of an art – much like the Song Dynasty ceramics. And by extremely skilled footwork, the great player knows just how to position himself or herself for maximum result, thus receiving positive Qi, or energy flow. Lastly, balance is of the utmost importance in a game played at such a fast pace, and the I Ching, as well as Taoism, are hinged on the principle of striking a balance between the opposing forces of Yin and Yang.

It seemed to us that eternal China was living on in its latest incarnation, and had much more to offer the world than material goods and pollution. So, we wondered, could one still find that iconic image from the past, aged philosophers living simply among surreal landscapes?

We weren't sure about that, but the surreal landscapes do exist, and are, therefore, real. We were gaping then at the outstanding karst peaks along the Li River in Southern China. One of the world's beauty spots, undoubtedly, but not exactly a secret. In fact, the dreamlike scenery is printed on the back of every twenty-Yuan bill. We were on the upper deck of a crowded, largish, diesel-belching ship in the middle of a long caravan of such vessels snaking slowly down the river. The ships were a spectacle in themselves: seasoned and rustic, astern they had an open-air kitchen in which cooks busied themselves to prepare the passengers' lunch just in time before docking in the town of Yangshuo.

After hectic mega- and mid-size cities (Xi'an, the ancient capital, is considered middle-sized – with a population of eight million), this was a respite. The scenery along the river, in the countryside and in the terraced rice fields was stunning. We met some westerners, among them a Hollywood film producer scouting for locations, and a couple of academics from Seattle with one camera and one lens too many. I mean, despite their elaborate equipment, four cases of it, were they getting the picture my wife and I were getting? They hardly had time to breathe between switching cameras and changing lenses while the beautiful scenery passed us by.

They all were enjoying their travels, but it was plain to see that China for them was not the Shangri-La it represented for me. Everywhere I looked, I couldn't help thinking: I bet that guy would give me a beating at table tennis. To make things worse, I had two untouched rackets in my hotel room, asleep in the darkness of their cases. First in Beijing and even more in Shanghai I'd wondered whether I should look for a TT club and drop by as a guest? But the prospect of playing against whom – champions? – had been too intimidating.

We'd decided to spend the last day shopping in the city of Guilin. The guide and chauffer turned up at the hotel after lunch. Before leaving with them I went to the restrooms by the lobby, and found a sign: *Table Tennis Room*, with an arrow. I went back to my wife and told her about it.

'Then you must!' she said. 'I'll see you later and, Guido, make me proud. *Zai jian.*'

'What does that mean?'

'See you.' A kiss, and off she went.

I went upstairs to our room to release my new rackets from the darkness and raced back downstairs, my legs propelled by acute table tennis craving. How long had it been since I had played?

The room was well appointed: large, high-ceilinged, well-lit, with three excellent tables and suitable flooring. And this is just for hotel guests, I thought. Some of them were playing then. I ever so slowly peeled off the protective film from the rubbers of my two new rackets, ever a moment full of promise.

Soon enough a man in his thirties asked me, the western oddity, if I wanted to play.

I started with the racket bought in Beijing, quickly realising that I didn't like it one bit. The carbon layers in the blade made it too jumpy. My control was not good. Every time I hit the ball, I didn't send it where I wanted; rather, I took a guess. I'll trade it for something else with some club member, back in DC, I thought as I switched to the other one.

In my hand was now Hurricane Hao, the blade used

by Wang Hao, and built to his specifications. It was love at first touch. Not as fast as I feared it would be, it had supreme control and fantastic touch. This was what I'd always been waiting for, the Platonic archetype for a blade. And the pre-tuned rubbers were impressive, too: extra spin and speed but not at the expense of control. It was instant karma. But how could that be? I asked myself with a regurgitation of linear thinking. Having played with the same combo for close to two years, any new combo should have thrown off my muscle memory. Well, for all it had served me up to then, I could throw the vaunted muscle memory that related to my previous racket in the gutter. But there was another possibility, and wonderfully nonlinear at that: what if my muscle memory had been remembering *forward* all along until it had finally chanced on the right racket, the one I was holding just then in my right hand? Mind-bending, true, but what else is new in the peculiar realm of table tennis?

My opponent was a pretty good player and I hadn't played for what seemed for ever, though it must have been a little over two weeks. But playing with Hurricane Hao after a hiatus was like drinking the coolest water after a long hike in the desert. Some strokes seemed to happen as it they had a will of their own.

The first player wasn't bad, schooled and all, but I didn't think he could have a rating much higher than 1400. I had better serves, spin, placement and loops. Sensing that this match was mine to win, I used it to explore the characteristics of my new combo. Some of my balls went long (the factory-tuned rubbers made it a faster combo than my previous one), and I had to calibrate my spins. All in all, I defeated my opponent fairly easily. If not shocked, he was certainly surprised.

I suppose the news spread quickly in the hotel. I was soon playing another match with a new opponent. This one reminded me of Kai, my first informal teacher at the community centre in which I had been initiated. He was perennially smiling, chubby, not tall and, I could tell as we warmed up, very consistent. This was going to be a challenge. The first player was clearly below my level, and I'd have beaten him anywhere, though perhaps not at Henry Miller's Memorial Library in California, if I'd been playing with a god-awful hardbat. But we were in China, and that simple but blunt notion was very intimidating. My challenging local players was nothing short of audacious, and it was probably perceived that way.

Kai's doppelgänger (I never got his name) would serve first. He had proposed – through gestures – to let luck decide who would go first, which is done routinely in table tennis: one player takes the ball, places both his hands under the table, passes the ball from one to the other, and then sets them apart; the opponent picks either hand; if he finds the ball in it, he serves first, and vice versa. But I'd felt chivalrous, and told him to start. Bad idea: he had a wicked serve, fast, to my backhand, very spinny.

I was down by a few points when I finally began to handle his serve. His style of play could be best defined as a wall. He returned just about everything but lacked, luckily for me, the killer instinct. The more I played him, the more he reminded me of Kai.

This match lasted longer, and was more involved, but I frequently succeeded in getting him out of position. He was sweating and panting heavily, which doesn't contribute to precise playing. In the end I won.

We shook hands: his was so squishy from sweating, it was like squeezing an eel. But there was nothing eel-like about him. He smiled at me, and I suppose he had a few words of praise for how I'd played – in China, from a Chinese player!

I smiled back, flattered, but still none too persuaded about my ability. Could it be all thanks to my new racket? It afforded me such control and precision, some of my shots seemed guided by telekinesis, literally 'distant-movement,' or the ability to move matter through the control of the mind. It's something all we TT players dream of, but it remains a dream. No, it must be the new racket.

I thought that it was high time to recognise the superior status of my Hurricane Hao and Skyline 3 Neo rubbers combo by giving it a name. I had felt all along that one's favourite combo should be given a name, much like knights in the Middle Ages used to give a name to their sword. The relationship with one's favourite combo is too exclusive and too close for it to be considered a mere 'tool.' My new racket, a case of both love at first touch *and* instant karma, deserved no less. I racked my brains thinking about a suitable name, while the Chinese players must have assumed I was trying to fish out from my memory different serves and unused shots in preparation for the next match. Then I decided for Durlindana, Italian for Durendal, the mythical sword of the paladin

Roland. And with that, I kissed it on both the forehand and the backhand side. Everybody looked at me enquiringly.

Players routinely blow some steam off their mouth onto their racket's rubbers during a match to get rid of the dust accumulated by touching the ball; but kiss it, that I don't think they'd seen before. I wanted to share this solemn moment with them so, pointing at my racket, I said solemnly: 'Durlindana!'

The western oddity was very much in character, they must have thought. And with that, I welcomed my new opponent, a woman.

Despite my euphoria over my two wins and my newly christened racket, I noticed that she was pretty – but 'that will not distract us, oh no,' I said looking at Durlindana. Or would it?

Back in the States, I'd seen Alex the Russian lose to every female opponent he played with simply because he was too chivalrous to beat women. It seemed, under the circumstances, a very good policy, always assuming that I was the better player, which was indeed an assumption, but that's the nature of hubris – the moment it sees an opportunity, it seizes it and sinks into us. I also wondered if Durlindana would mind my losing on purpose out of chivalry? Of course not! Besides, 'It's only a game, only a game,' I told myself – and my racket.

Furthermore, I was a guest in their country; all Chinese we'd met had been so welcoming and accommodating; the whole country was cheerful and hospitable; I'd had two wins already in the Holy Land of Table Tennis; I could leave it at that – why insist? What for? And did this young woman have to be so gracefully petite? Maybe we could just train, no match, no points. Should I ask her? Yes, there was the language barrier, but we both spoke the lingua franca of TT. I went over to her side to ask, and caught a glimpse of her racket.

What do we have here? I wondered in my mind, taken aback. A-ha, long pips on one side, the tricky empiricist!

No matter how petite and graceful, I had a strong hunch that she was going to give me hell – and make a laughing stock of me in front of everyone – me, the western oddity who kissed his racket and called it by name. My beating her wasn't at all a given. I smiled at my previous conciliatory thoughts, but she must have thought that I was smiling at her, and smiled back. She *was* pretty, but I made the resolution that 'neither that nor her long pips will distract us.'

I was warm already, in fact sweating from the previous matches, but I allowed her to warm up. This is ordinary TT etiquette, nothing to do with being chivalrous. I could already tell that she was good; typically, though, she was hitting nothing with her backhand, where she had the long-pips rubber. Empiricists are made with a mould, I thought. They don't touch a single ball with their long-pips side during the warm-up, thinking that that way they'll have an ace up their sleeve during the match. If the opponent is unaware of their having long pips on one side, this stratagem can win them a few points, till the opponent figures out what's going on. If, on the other hand, the opponent has inspected their racket beforehand, it's an insult to his intelligence. Did she think I was going to forget that she was an empiricist?

She served.

She was agile and quite technical, not at all a passive defender like Pedro. She returned with her long-pips backhand only to get in a favourable position from which to unleash her forehand loop. There was quite a number of people watching us by then. They must have thought that the odd westerner had found his match.

I lost the first game, and then the second, too, but this one cost her a great deal of work. Part of the blame for my poor performance fell on Durlindana. With it I could create unprecedented amounts of spin, but all that topspin would be reversed by the young woman's long pips, and came straight back at me as the most backspinned balls I'd ever experienced. It was a dilemma. If I didn't loop, *she* would loop. If I did loop, I'd be creating very backspinned balls that gave me a lot of trouble. Lifting the ball with my loop was hard, and more often than not I'd send the ball into the net.

Jaime had explained to me what to do against such players, and demonstrated it against Pedro, by . . . destroying him. Loop after loop, until Pedro could no longer cope. 'So,' I said to myself as we were getting ready for the third game, 'it boils down to placing yet more topspin on my loops, and looping the hell out of her long pips.' It was a matter of concentration, patience and . . . strength. It takes a lot of strength to lift many heavily backspinned balls in a row, and I had to win three games in a row if I wanted to have a successful comeback.

It must have seemed grotesque to see a six-foot tall man unleash all his power against a petite young woman. And to think that I'd had reservations about beating her! Well, she didn't have to be an empiricist and play with long pips. The one I was adopting is the only strategy that will do away with a skilled long-pips player. There's no other way.

I was fighting for every ball, sweating from my every pore, and trying to catch my breath between points. I realised that I was letting her balls drop very low so as to give my forehand loops a yet ampler movement, one that began about a foot and a half from the floor and ended above my eyes. Exhausting and in my view not exactly elegant, but it was working.

After a long struggle I won the third game, to everybody's surprise, judging from the expression on their faces. Then I got into a cadenced looping rhythm, changed my grip slightly, and the loops came a little more easily to me. It gradually became like playing against the robot at Jaime's house; there was nothing to it other than technique, timing, and quite a lot of physical exertion.

The fourth game was mine too, with less of a struggle, and in the fifth game she capitulated, letting me win by a wide margin.

'We did it!' I said to Durlindana.

I went over to shake hands with her, and I was met with the same look I'd first known at the Chinese Club back in the States: she stared at me as if she were in awe. Had she spoken English, I suspect she would have said, 'You're good, you're *really* good . . .'

All this had a pernicious effect on me, producing a cocktail of bloated self-esteem and euphoria. In such a state, I remembered barely noticing that my opponents wouldn't leave, nor would they start a match on the other tables. They stuck around, watching all my matches.

I must have been playing for a couple of hours with few interruptions, mainly to drink, and drink again.

Eventually a small crowd formed. This is too precious, I thought; they were here to watch the *rara avis*, the 'strange bird' from the West, and I guess one way or the other I was making a fine spectacle of myself. First, I had been a chicken, too timid to step into a proper TT club and try out my new equipment with some advanced player. Now, after a few unexpected wins in a hotel TT hall, my hubris must have grown a comb on top of my head, and I must have looked like an oversized rooster – a strange bird indeed.

After yet another win with a thankfully mediocre player, I went to drink, this time Coca-Cola; I needed the sugar, the caffeine and especially the bubbles, to feel even more buoyant.

Coming back all bubbled up I found a young man waiting for me. Eyeing me appraisingly, he said something in Mandarin; two bystanders translated: 'Would you like to play with him?'

'Sure,' I said, and added in my mind, Bring it on!

Even during the warm-up I could tell that this was no casual player. I doubt that he was a hotel guest at all, more probably some sort of resident champion who had been summoned for the occasion because of my previous wins. I'll never know, but the thought was flattering.

He was a traditional penholder, using the forehand as his main stroke. Unlike the world champion Liu Guoliang, who pioneered the reverse backhand later perfected by his successor Wang Hao, this player resorted to the backhand sparingly, only to block or push. Instead, he would step around the ball to hit it with his forehand, but was as fast as a cat and as strong as a bear. All in all, I estimated him at 300 or even 400 above my rating.

There was no way I could beat this player. The comb on my head receded and quickly disappeared as the bubble of bloated self-esteem, euphoria and hubris burst.

I could casually look at my watch and pretend to be late for something or other. But the subterfuge seemed as inglorious as playing with long pips. Well, at least I was lucid again, all exaggerated evaluations of myself gone, back where I belonged, and that is, on the losing side. Because lose I would, my fate was sealed.

Or was it?

As we kept warming up, my mind was thinking frantically. I remembered reading somewhere about the 'anti-karmic' measures adopted sometimes in traditional cultures. Among the ancient Romans, for example, the augur was an official in charge of interpreting omens for guidance in public affairs, and most urgently in war. The general would consult the augur, and then act according to the augury. If the augury was unpropitious, the general could still choose to move into battle, but would take extra measures: change strategy, call for reinforcements, employ different weapons, and so on. It was a daring way of contrasting fate, or karma, with, precisely, anti-karmic measures.

Now, the karma was firmly on my opponent's side. This was his game to lose. What could I do to outwit what was written in the stars: my defeat? I had no clue. Also because the more we played, the more formidable an opponent he seemed. We were using six brand-new three-star balls for the warm-up and within minutes he had broken two of them by smashing them too vehemently. If this display of both force and dexterity (since his balls did land on the table) was supposed to impress me, it was succeeding. I might get lucky: if he kept this up, we may run out of balls.

But no such luck, as he finally said something. Translation: 'I'm ready when you are.'

'Let's start,' I said, and added in my mind, And get it over with.

He said something else. 'Do you want to play four games out of seven?'

Like at the Olympics, I thought. What the hell, I might as well go out with a bang. So I said in Mandarin that I wanted to: '*Yào.*'

He returned my first serve into the net. An auspicious beginning or beginner's luck?

The first game was very even. As an anti-karmic measure, I gave him a few of my 'cross-fertilised' stokes. I had risked my discipleship and friendship with Jaime over such strokes. He, the purist, was all against them; I was only too proud of having invented them, assuming I had, of which I'm not at all certain. They consist of mixing shakehand (western-style) strokes with penhold (Asian-style) ones. In other words, by playing so much with Chinese penholders, I have adopted some of their shots, which I execute with my shakehand grip. Jaime abhors them – 'junk ping-pong' – and would prefer that I used conventional strokes in their stead. But, since I've never seen anyone use them, they're good *surprise* shots. After many discussions, some of them intense, Jaime and I had reached a compromise: whatever is over the table, anything goes; but the strokes from mid-distance and away from the table, those must be conventional ones, simply because only such strokes are effective and consistent.

With a fairly good player, I can milk a few points out of my cross-fertilised shots: being so unusual and surprising, the opponent doesn't know what's coming at him or her. With this player, I got one point out of each, and never tried again, knowing that their disorienting effect would be over after the first time, and in themselves they're *not* formidable. That gave me an edge, though, and I won the first game. My fate, perhaps, was not sealed. Hail to those risk-taking generals from ancient Rome: risk must be a prerequisite of empire-building.

But it was too soon to crow, silly me and my rooster-like impetuses.

I remember vaguely how the second game went. I was at times out of breath, and sweating profusely all the time. I played short and backspinned, which visibly annoyed him. Had I opened the game to rallies of topsins, he would've eaten me alive, of that I was sure. This wasn't his game, and sometimes he would be caught out of position. Only then would I loop, or drive, and score. Also, my backhand was superior to his simply because he didn't really have one, so I insisted in playing on his backhand side, too. To be sure, mine was a wholly un-heroic approach, one that consisted, in essence, of disarming him, but the worst thing I could have done was pretend that I could play at his level.

With a supreme effort of concentration, I managed to win this game too, just barely. A voice inside me was saying, *He's just studying you, you'll see*, and at any moment I expected him to shift gear and, in two words, destroy me.

He was a looper of the consummate type. He'd loop once, and get me slightly out of position; twice, and I'd be definitely out of position; finally, he'd place a 'loop-kill,' with a flatter arc, faster and more spinny yet, as the put-away ball, and score. A simple plan, but the execution was flawless, and the simple is very difficult to actualise. I had the impression that so far he'd been holding back.

It was more than an impression. In the third game he took the lead and never let me catch up. I'd run out of anti-karmic measures, and it was surprising that they should have worked in the first place. The small crowd that was watching was cheering my opponent – as if he needed encouragement – and I could see them gloating in antici-pation of my being soundly beaten. I felt tired, thirsty, hungry. Who did I think I was, to accept the challenge of such a better player? I was going to be ridiculed.

Which, come to think of it, Chinese players just don't do. In my experience in playing against them in the States, they're very matter-of-fact and sportsmanlike. They just play as well as they can. Win or lose, they always shake hands at the end, neither obnoxious winners nor sore losers.

And precisely with that matter-of-fact approach my opponent easily took the third game.

And then the fourth.

Out of the corner of my eye I saw my wife enter the room then, bags in her hands. Not now! I thought. That she would turn up just in time to see me lose, that was awful. If only she'd come back earlier; I'd had such a good run . . . Of course now that she was here, I'd try not just to hold my own and score some points, but to impress her.

Wrong idea: the fifth game began with my losing four points in a row. As I sweated and gave it my all, I kept getting flashes of Jaime's teachings: 'Stay low! Control! Finish the movement! Lean forward! Get in position! Don't jump!' How stupid could I be? Why hadn't I internalised his teachings yet? Why did I need to *think* about them? I so wanted to impress my wife, who had not seen me play competitive TT since the beginning of my obsession, but I conceded the fifth game, too.

I caught a glimpse, then, of the pretty young woman I'd defeated. She was one of the few not cheering my opponent. Perhaps, if I'd won, it would have made her loss against me more bearable. Perhaps, apart from skilful, graceful and pretty, she was also a gentlewoman, and kept her feelings to herself.

I had to win the sixth game, and then the seventh. Easier said than done: all the advantages were my opponent's – psychological, technical, and the supporters were by now rooting for him deafeningly. Many of them, some probably from outside the hotel.

Come on, I thought, give me some slack, will you? I'm just a western oddity, half-chicken, half-rooster.

My opponent was very well trained, with impressive biceps and a muscular structure to match. The over-trained becomes muscle-bound, I said to myself, half-believing it.

My wife was looking at me calmly as I wiped off the sweat from my forehead. I knew what she was thinking: You can do it, Guido. You can do it.

And with that began the sixth game.

I hit shots that I didn't think I could hit. I exchanged my cautious approach for a much bolder one, with many parallel loops to his backhand side. I should have been doing so all along: the new, factory-tuned rubbers consistently developed very heavy spin, and in addition to that possibly by now I was getting my second wind. Was my body suddenly producing endorphins? Or was it finding the right balance of oxygen to counteract the accumulation of lactic acid in my muscles? Or neither? I had no clue, but suddenly I felt not so tired any more, and a little more confident. Maybe my wife, with her positive energy, had broken the spell, or if nothing else the balance of support, which had been all in my opponent's favour.

He was sweating as much as I was, and whenever he scored a point, he let out a loud scream, echoed by the crowd. He hadn't being doing that before, which meant that he now feared me. When I scored, on the other hand, I saved my breath and kept my cool, which, although I didn't realise it at the time, must have been interpreted by my opponent as a sign of self-assurance.

We went to deuce, and he was visibly angry about that.

After an interminable see-saw – his advantage, deuce, my advantage, deuce, and so on and on – I dared to hit a diagonal loop-kill, to his forehand. After sending loops to his backhand for the whole match, he didn't expect one there. He still could have reached it, only to unleash a devastating counterloop, but I had added a little hook (sidespin fading out) for insurance: that couple of extra inches to the side made it unreachable though, with uncharacteristic loss of form, he had dived to his right side in an attempt to reach it, and had fallen.

I'd won the sixth game, and that last loop had not only given me the game, but made quite an impression, with my opponent falling on the floor.

My wife Stenie was cheering me while the suddenly quiet crowd looked on, nonplussed.

We'd now won three games each. The seventh game would be the tie-breaker.

We both went to drink and dry our hands, arms, faces and necks before continuing. I could have drunk a whole gallon, but that would have taken time and somehow I wanted to get back to the table and get it over with. If this was a momentum-breaker, it was more so for me than for him.

When we got back I saw that somebody had wiped the

table clean of our sweat. Somebody else had provided us with a set of brand-new, three-star balls.

With my first serve, I noticed something strange: I no longer heard outside noises. That's something that happens to me when I play more than three hours in a row: somehow my ears become plugged. I had them checked by an otolaryngologist, and nothing seems to be wrong with them. Might it be that after so much exertion I start sweating from the *inside*? Anyway, this time they were more plugged than usual, so that my hearing became internalised: I heard only my breathing, the sound of the balls I hit, even my heart, racing.

The initial phase of the seventh and last game was my opponent's. Then what intruded into my mind was not Jaime with his teachings but, of all things, a Cuban song. It was '*El Manicero*,' 'The Peanut Vendor,' no doubt about that. I didn't know why this was happening, but happening it was, and it felt refreshing. I was hearing it loud and clear in Spanish; in English, it goes: 'In Cuba, his smiling face / Is welcome most every place / Peanuts! They hear him cry / Peanuts! They all reply,' and so on. Emilio, my almost octogenarian Cuban friend, came to mind. Surely this most famous of Cuban songs must have been blaring through the loudspeakers when I was playing at his house. Emilio . . . and then it dawned on me: I could try a strategy inspired by his style.

Emilio plays very close to the table, anticipating the opponent's every stroke by letting the ball just barely bounce. That could work, I thought, and began to 'hug' the table.

This is counterintuitive: my opponent's loops were so fast and spinny, my natural reaction, even after so much training and after playing six games against him, was to back away from the table. But that's Jaime's biggest no-no: 'For Heaven's sake, don't go back!'

I stayed so close to the table, I almost touched it. This way, I blocked my opponent's formidable loops as soon as they hit the table. They hardly had time to bounce. I was thus minimising his topspins, blocking them back and making him run to either side of the table. It reminded me of a drill I do with Jaime to improve my mobility and footwork, except this time *I* was the one blocking and making the opponent run.

Some balls he just missed, other he returned too vehemently, losing his cool and with it his accuracy. They landed out.

Others yet, he ended up lifting and then *I* was the one driving them from over the net. I even broke one.

I had caught up but, for all my strategising, it was still a very close game.

The Cuban song had faded, and my internalised hearing with it: I was now hearing normally, but not paying attention to any sound other than that of the ball. It was as if three years of competitive TT training and decades of studying eastern and western esotericism had alchemically distilled in a single atom, or better, a single 2.7-gram, 40-mm diameter oxygen-filled celluloid ball.

The end was approaching. The score was, incredibly, 10–8 in my favour, and it was my turn to serve. I had two match balls at my disposal.

This is where I lose the match, said a diabolical little voice inside me. As soon as I served, I realised that I had fumbled: he looped once, twice, and with the third loop the ball flew away from me after bouncing to my left side.

10–9.

My second serve.

I decided to think something, consciously, just to silence that self-sabotaging voice inside me. *Durlindana*, I said in my mind addressing my racket, *forgive my inadequacy and please guide my hand for this last point*. That 'last point' boldly implied that I would score, otherwise there'd be more points to contend.

A pause followed.

In complete silence, I concentrated more than I ever had, then served a 'double-bouncer,' a short serve that, if left untouched, would bounce twice on the opponent's side of the table. Nothing out of the ordinary about that; it had just a touch of sidespin, to his left, but no backspin. From the movement I had made, though, it seemed that there was also *backspin* on the ball. It was the first time I did this in all seven games. He 'opened' his racket to compensate for the *perceived* backspin and returned the ball to my forehand. The room was so quiet, one could have heard a pin drop. Sure enough, they heard something drop: my opponent's ball, but on the floor, long, and out.

I looked at him, then at my wife, then all around: I had won.

There was consternation on everyone's face but then, astonishingly, they began to clap, me, the strange bird from the West!

Stenie came up to me smiling broadly, kissed me, and said: 'There you go, well done! I knew you could do it!'

I was dripping and there was a pool of sweat by my feet. I looked at my opponent. The match point I had won by cleverness, but had played all the games openly, relying on technique and concentration. Or had I?

My opponent came over to my side of the table to shake hands. He said something that was promptly translated: 'Good game, you've won fair and square.'

'Thank you,' I replied, and thought, impressed, Oh my, that was gracious of him.

Everybody was still clapping, and the women, with the pretty petite one among them, were now giving me that look I knew so well from the Chinese club back in the States: 'You're *good* . . .'

Postlude

The night after that memorable afternoon in Guilin I had trouble falling asleep. I kept reliving in my mind the highlights of the various matches, especially the one against the petite young woman and then against the resident champion, assuming that that's what he was. I came up with a number of reasons for my wins, but could easily have come up with as many reasons for *losing*, especially the last match. What seemed a plausible explanation dawned on me well after midnight: perhaps rather than striving for transcendence, trying constantly to rise above myself, for once I had more modestly and more realistically concentrated on immanence, from the Latin *in manere* – to remain within.

But even as we were flying from Shanghai back to the States I realised that I'd been generous in the appraisal of my performance. If Jaime had been present during the last match, after a few games he'd have left the room, considering me a lost cause. I was all over the place, nothing to do with balancing the Yin and Yang to let the Tao flow, as the Chinese would have it. True, some of my playing was unexpectedly brilliant, but some just awful with hints of slapstick in it, and everything in between. In fact, this schizophrenic style might have helped: the opponent never knew what to expect. Perhaps he thought that I was alternating good moments to terrible ones to confuse or deceive him. Flattering, but I'm no Sun Tzu: I was just trying to cope with his higher standards of play. I barely won, and knew full well that, had we played again, *he* would have won, simply because *he* was the better player. I had a long way to go, and beating an advanced Chinese player on his own turf had paradoxically made me more aware of this.

In the *Tao Te Ching*, Lao Tzu states: 'For to those who have conformed themselves to the Way, the Way readily lends its power. To those who have conformed themselves to the power, the power readily lends more power. While to those who conform themselves to inefficacy, inefficacy readily lends its ineffectiveness.'

The higher the level of table tennis, the more its champions have conformed themselves to the Way (the Te). Te is a key concept of Taoism. Roughly, it is one's integrity, not in the western sense of honour, but in the psychological sense of a full integration of who one is. Te is self-nature and, in relation to the cosmos, self-realisation. The cosmic principle actualises itself in the self. Each creature has a Te, its own expression of the Tao. Precisely this interrelationship between the Tao and the Te is the secret of the superior man or woman. And then there's the matter of 'con-forming,' that is, literally, to be with the *form*. Platonic pure form, again, is what one must aspire to. As explained previously, this is a universal principle, one that echoes from Plato's to Lao Tzu's words. Down the millennia, the Perennial Philosophy has produced strikingly similar concepts even if expressed in different ways.

The more I thought about my memorable match, the more I realised how out of harmony I'd been throughout it. 'But you won,' the materialist would argue, 'and in the end that's all that counts.' Well, yes, it *was* a major upset, and beating an advanced Chinese player on his own turf had felt sensational, I won't deny that. But in a tournament context, a 'conforming' and well-balanced player such as my opponent would have beaten me. Curious things will happen, and perhaps in that recreational context my opponent overestimated the gap between the two of us, or simply didn't play as consistently as he normally would.

An initiatic axiom of our own western tradition states: 'You must not seek power; it's power that must seek you.' In the esoteric tradition, power is feminine, and is looking for a centre. 'Through domination of his own soul, by isolation and resistance, the initiate will attract power;' 'she' will obey him as her own male. In table tennis world-class players give the illusion of *not* chasing the ball: the opposite seems to happen. Perhaps it's more than an illusion, and it takes something other than mere persistence to get there.

What could I do to get to that *dimension*, rather than *level*?

Back in the States I found websites clamouring to have the answer. Mental training, self-hypnosis, let your subconscious mind take over and control all your body movements. Subconscious mind? If I've ever known an initiatic discipline firsthand, that is table tennis. It's a constant struggle uphill, towards top form and peak performances. 'Uphill,' 'top' and 'peak,' I just wrote; emphasising one's *sub*conscious, and that is, things known *below* one's consciousness, negates this principle. The whole *telos* – a Greek word that in philosophy stands for goal, finality, though 'projectuality' renders the idea better – is to *elevate* one's technique until not only does it reach a very high level, but in fact trespasses into another dimension, one in which eternal balances of energy and power come into play. The subconscious knows absolutely nothing about this, and no higher level, let alone realm, could ever be produced by it.

Then there was the problem of too much thinking, too many thoughts crowding my mind while I play, instructions, pointers, and so on. The intellect clouds the picture. Jaime has been even too patient with me. I should internalise all his teachings and then throw them away once and for all. There's nothing that he would like more than to play with me as equals. Which is, I suppose, what happened when Jalal ad-Din Rumi and Shams Tabrizi met.

Rumi was one of the most learned and respected jurists of his time. One day he was sitting in his personal library. Students were gathered around him for a lecture. Suddenly, a raggedy old man, Shams, entered uninvited. He pointed to the books and asked Rumi: 'What are these?'

Rumi answered: 'You would not understand.' As soon as he finished speaking, flames rose from the books. Frightened, he cried out: 'What is it?'

Shams replied, calmly: 'Nor would you understand this.'

From that day on, Shams became Rumi's spiritual teacher, and Rumi one of the most beloved mystics and poets of all time. Does this mean that his poems were composed with the same skills of an illiterate child? Not at all; it certainly helped his poetry that he was learned, but he had finally *transcended* mere learning.

Chuang Tzu expresses the same concept through different words: 'The fish trap exists because of the fish. Once you've got the fish you can forget the trap. The rabbit snare exists because of the rabbit. Once you've got the rabbit, you can forget the snare. Words exist because of meaning. Once you've got the meaning, you can forget the words. Where can I find a man who has forgotten words so I can talk with him?'

It's a simple message: enough academic learning. Rules and laws can take you only so far, but never beyond the threshold. Once you've assimilated them so well that you know them inside out, you can free yourself of them, and enter a higher dimension.

I've seen Jaime play with opponents of his level, and admired professional players during tournaments; I saw the provincial team players train in Beijing a few feet away from me; YouTube teems with videos of the world's top players competing in the most important tournaments. I'm persuaded that none of these exceptionally accomplished players think at all while they play. But I won't trivialise their arrived-at state of grace by putting it down to their persistence in training, their subconscious, their muscle memory, or any of such reductionist explanation. That's why I wrote 'state of grace.'

According both to the mystics of different cultures and to psychology, grace is beyond our self-conscious – and even less so our subconscious – self. It's capable of being of help to us. Animal grace comes when we're in perfect harmony with our nature by living wholesomely, with no abuses or cravings. Such a state of harmony with the Tao, in the East, or with the Logos – the cosmological principle that governs and develops the universe – in the West, results in a sense of well-being and a perception of life as being good and worth living. Then there's human grace, which comes to us from fellow human beings. In the sphere of table tennis, one can speak about the grace of the coach, which he passes on to his student. Finally there's spiritual grace, which we may think belongs exclusively to saints or particularly enlightened persons, but that's not the case. It comes from without ourselves or other persons, and may be perceived as being 'on loan,' as the sixteenth-century Christian mystic St John of the Cross wrote.

In my view, the world–class TT champion is fully invested by animal grace as well as human grace, the latter not just in terms of what they receive from their coach, but also from their fans. Occasionally, during a high–level memorable match, one or both players seem to go beyond the high standards of their playing, beyond the help afforded by animal and human grace, to enter into a state of spiritual grace. Taoists would say that the champions are then overflowing with Te, through which the Tao is not only manifesting but also actualising itself. Westerners would say, as sports commentators sometimes *do* say, that they're in a state of grace – and with good reason. In other words, they've entered what Plato called the World of Forms.

Table tennis of that dimension can be seen as the harmless re-enactment of primeval battles between archetypal agents. The fact that nobody gets hurt since it's not a contact sport doesn't mean that through it we can't see a clash between forces much greater than even the greatest athlete. This spiritual and cosmological dimension of table tennis makes it only natural that it should be played at its very best in East-Asian countries, where for centuries martial arts have been at once athletic and esoteric disciplines. And the western players who, in the last decades, have excelled in the sport have, for the vast majority, trained in China, too, thus coming in contact not only with coaches and training techniques, but also with the culture as a whole.

Having said that, it's true that sometimes also athletes from the western world treat us to such extraordinary performances that we call them 'epic.' It's not journalistic rhetoric, because occasionally such athletes seem to go beyond the very best that they could realistically expect from themselves, and step up to previously unknown territories. In all likelihood they're experiencing a 'state of grace' – animal, human and spiritual. The difference between western and East-Asian TT players is that the latter are seeking the Tao *consciously*, or at least trying to. But the conscious summoning of a state of grace is no easy feat, and that's why it's rarely achieved on command, otherwise all high-level matches would be 'epic,' and they aren't. A short story by Chuang Tzu expresses what some of us may not like to hear.

Shun asked Ch'êng, saying: 'Can one get Tao so as to have it for one's own?'

'Your very body,' replied Ch'êng, 'is not your own. How should Tao be?'

'If my body,' said Shun, 'is not my own, pray whose is it?'

'It is the delegated image of God,' replied Ch'êng. 'Your life is not your own. It is the delegated harmony of God. Your individuality is not your own. It is the delegated adaptability of God. Your posterity is not your own. It is the delegated exuviae of God. You move, but know not how. You are at rest, but know not why. You taste, but know not the cause. These are the operation of God's laws. How then should you get Tao so as to have it for your own?'

When a few years back I picked up a racket, or rather a hardbat, at Henry Miller's Memorial Library in Big Sur, California, I certainly didn't suspect a number of things. That I'd be soundly beaten by my teenage son; that shortly thereafter I'd become obsessed with table tennis; that my obsession would fuel a gruelling initiation that, in a sense, is still going on today; that the sport itself would reacquaint me with some eternal principles of the Perennial Philosophy and afford me new glimpses of sempiternal wisdom; that it'd teach me so much about myself, our human condition and life; and that, finally, in 'humble' table tennis I'd be looking for the living presence that informs the phenomenal world. But why shouldn't I? The spinning ball is our Planet Earth.

I still play with the combo I bought half the Earth away from where I live, in Shanghai. I replace the rubbers periodically but with the exact same type, and still call that particular racket Durlindana. I'm ashamed to say that from time to time I've betrayed *her* by trying some new combo, only to realise how much I was missing Durlindana and go back to her with my tail between my legs. There's something angelic about chancing on one's perfect match as there's something diabolic in constantly trying to find a better one yet.

So much of what I've experienced since my true beginnings finds such echoes in archetypal images and motifs that it'd be foolish to ignore them. As for learning, both about the sport and about all that's behind it and beyond it, that was and continues to be fun. I certainly could have done without the initial hundreds of defeats, but, at my age, there was no way around that, and mercifully most of my early opponents were gracious rather than conceited. Every week there was a new discovery, and the deriving enthusiasm kept me going. It's helped that I've got better at it, but it's now clear to me and hopefully to you too that proficiency per se is not the ultimate goal. Besides, there's a lot left for me to learn and then, hopefully, there will be a lot for me to *unlearn*.

Lin Yutang was a philosopher of life, a translator of Chinese classics into English, a novelist and an inventor. He is, for example, the one who finally solved the riddle and, in 1946, succeeded in producing the unthinkable: a workable Chinese typewriter. Amid his writings he left many epigrams, lustrous exercises in informal and witty prose as well as in nonlinear thinking. And one of such pearls I like to place at the end of these pages.

'A good traveller is one who does not know where he is going to, and a perfect traveller does not know where he came from.'

Acknowledgements

M any thanks to:
Christopher Sinclair-Stevenson, for his friendship, for encouraging me to write this book, and for reading it in its various incarnations.

Gardner Monks, for his friendship since our days in film school together; for escorting me to Ecuador with his brother Charles while doing research for another book; and for reading the various drafts and offering many enlightening comments.

My co-author Joscelyn Godwin and fellow player Rupert Sheldrake, for the many embracive discussions about the *Philosophia perennis* and the *Mundus imaginalis*.

Emilio Bernal Labrada, for introducing me to the world of (real) table tennis and for being the most *simpatico* man I know.

Jaime Álvarez, for being the *conditio sine qua non* of my every progress in table tennis, and for being so exceptionally patient and – along with his wife Doris and their children Stephanie and Alex – so welcoming.

The philosopher and historian of philosophy Riccardo Pozzo, for reading the manuscript and offering his anti-metaphysical counterpoint à la Montaigne's '*Je ne définis rien.*'

Clio Mitchell for all her musings (*nomen, omen*) and Ken Kubernik for our impassioned exchanges of ideas.

Everybody at the Northern Virginia Table Tennis Club (NVTTC) in Arlington, and in particular: Tom Norwood, President and personification of the southern gentleman; Fred Siskind, Vice-President and economist extraordinaire; Mike McCormick, Treasurer, gentleman farmer and keen reader; John Papp, Secretary and practitioner of the subtlest humour.

The four men I've called 'giants of the human spirit': Alex Muchnik, the kindest of Russian bears and IT wizard, who gave me the PC on which I've written this book and fine-tuned it for me constantly. Joseph Segal, most personable and loquacious man and enabler of much of my zaniness, especially when we played as a duo. Gilbert Delos Angeles, terrific player with the greatest sense of humour. And Hieng, a visiting guest whose surname I've never known.

And then, in alphabetical order: Wassim Alami, Eugene Amobi, George Anderson, Peter Andrews, Carlos Antunes, Carlos Arnade, Edgar Bailiff, Eric Bolz, Mike Brown – the former President, Peter Campbell, Jose Ceballos, Ying Chen, Carlos Contreras, Georgina de Wilde, Nelson Egbert, Kangfei Gan, Adil Gibrel, Mirek Gorski, Xiangmei Gu, Joseph Hawkins, Sokoma Heng, Jon Hiratsuka, Bill Horn, Peter Jacobi, Houman Jalali, David James, Bijan

Katebini, Venkata Krishna, 'Jenny' Chan Lang, Paul Le, Wu Ji Li, David Lovins, Ryan Luu, Adnan Madi, Enrique Matta, Deapesh Misra, John Mitchell, Larry Mooney, Ibrahim Nassef, Tam Nguyen, Sami Omer, Nihal Parekh, Ivan Patcherezov, Liang Peng, Kim Phan, Praveen Ravi, Gerald Rhoads, Wael Sherman, John Shew, Jozef Simkovic, Kishore Sirvole, Kenneth Spitz, Randy Stump, Margarita Tadenosyan, Lawrence Tan, Yon Wacker, Ye Wang, Jeff Xu, Min Xu, Kyle Yen, Fei Zhao, Pete Zombori.

And last but not least, Harbin Li, for his priceless mix of lucidity and lunacy, and for inadvertently illustrating, often vividly, various differences between the East and the West.

The father and son duo – Mr Lu Senior and Junior – of the Northern Virginia Table Tennis Center, in Chantilly (the 'Chinese club'), and all the players there, some of whom migrated from the community centre in which I was originally initiated, including Kai, who has since left the area.

Everybody at the Potomac Country Table Tennis Club I and II, respectively in Potomac and Cabin John, Maryland.

Everybody at Club JOOLA, in Rockville, Maryland.

Everybody at the Pasadena Table Tennis Club, in Pasadena, California.

Everybody at SPiN, in New York City.

Every opponent I've played with in America, Europe and Asia and whose name I have not asked.

My agent Gillon Aitken for everything, and for being the marvellous man that he is; the wonderful Sally Riley, and everyone at Aitken Alexander Associates.

Rachel Cugnoni for taking on this project, and Frances Jessop for her many insightful suggestions, for her enthusiasm and for her tender loving care.

Index